and Man

1295

Speech and Man

CHARLES T. BROWN / CHARLES VAN RIPER
Western Michigan University

PRENTICE-HALL, INC. Englewood Cliffs, New Jersey

Current printing (last digit):

10 9 8 7 6 5 4 3 2

Library of Congress Catalog Card No.: 66-17164
Printed in the United States of America (82745-C)

PRENTICE-HALL INTERNATIONAL, INC., *London*
PRENTICE-HALL OF AUSTRALIA, PTY. LTD., *Sydney*
PRENTICE-HALL OF CANADA, LTD., *Toronto*
PRENTICE-HALL OF INDIA (PRIVATE) LTD., *New Delhi*
PRENTICE-HALL OF JAPAN, INC., *Tokyo*

This book is dedicated to Russell Seibert,
Vice President of Western Michigan University,
who made its birth possible in an old hunting
cabin in the wilds of Northern Michigan.

Preface

This book was written to serve, not as a major text for a skills course in speech, but as its pleasant companion. We have long felt that the students in our courses were seeking something more than we were giving them. We knew they wanted to feel comfortable and effective when facing their listeners, but even when we managed to help them become so, they still seemed to want more. In exploring the matter it became clear that when we touched on the deeper purposes served by our speaking, which this book seeks to make clear, our students responded with the excited interest that all instructors hope to arouse. Deep down, all of us know that speech is the most important single achievement of the human race, the most powerful magic that man has invented. It is the open sesame to self-fulfillment, the basic bond that unites us one to another. We talk so much, so casually, so often that we tend at times to forget the power we possess through speech. Yet it is this very sense of possessing a tremendously powerful tool without knowing quite how to use it that brings students, often reluctantly, to enroll in our courses. We have designed this book for them.

Moreover, that speech education which rests in the liberal arts tradition and hopes to prepare the oncoming generation to act with wisdom in the precarious years ahead must stir the student to feel the role of speech in life and to sense the power of words, both for good and for evil. The following pages describe the incredibly complicated speech act, its many functions, and how speech, when developed, helps us gain some mastery of our puny lives in the powerful social forces that sometimes seem to engulf us. The instructor may want to refer to this volume at times in his assignments and evaluations. He may want to discuss certain parts with the class. He may want to lecture on certain ideas, or to augment them, or to contradict them, or even to condemn them. He may merely want his students to read the book.

We have based our discourse on the mass of accumulating research in the behavioral sciences, on our experiences as persons and teachers, and on an overriding sense of man's desperate need to grasp greater command of his potential. Over the years we have observed that growth and speech development are inextricably entwined, and we try to show that speech training is the most direct and the most effective approach to opening or closing the possibilities of a human life.

It was difficult to know how to begin this book, and harder yet to stop, for speech is as complex and as many faceted as the human who uses it. But we decided that first we should seek to demonstrate that very complexity so that the miracle of the moving mouth might be properly appreciated. Accordingly, in the first chapter we devote our discussion to a review of the basic features of speech: the motoric, the acoustic, and the linguistic. That being done, we open the doors to the basic functions with which speech serves its master, man. We begin by portraying its potential power for solving our emotional problems. We next show its usefulness in the search for personal identity. Then, in turn, we reveal how man uses speech to communicate, to control, and to think. Finally, believing as Oscar Wilde did that the only way to get rid of a temptation is to yield to it, we end our essay with a brief piece on the pleasures of speech. We hope the ideas will intrigue you as they did us in their implication for the training of the youth of tomorrow.

Charles T. Brown
Charles Van Riper

Contents

Speech and Man

1 The Miracle of Speech

In the second century after the birth of Christ, Ptolemy, a Greek astronomer living in Egypt, described his universe as a series of stars and planets continuously circling the earth. He wrote of the "music of the spheres," a cosmic hum that only the gods might hear. We know now that he was wrong, but surely this earth buzzes continuously with one sound at least—the sound of human speech. At this very moment, millions upon millions of people are talking, some of them even in their sleep. Speech is the most unique and the most universal of human functions, yet, because it is so commonplace, so natural, so easy, few of us appreciate its enormous power and potential. It is our supreme tool, but like the ape who employs a flute to scratch himself, we have not yet learned all the uses of this greatest of human inventions. Only a handful of us ever learn to use this tool for more than the most primitive of its functions; to that handful we give the fruits of the earth and our worship. Consider how barren our histories of civilization would be had our great men never learned to talk.

Because speaking is so commonplace, only those who have been deprived of normal utterance seem to appreciate its magical power. The stutterer, struggling desperately to answer a casual question, knows. The cancer patient whose larynx has been removed finds suddenly that all existence has changed because the air pressure that once permitted speech to emerge from his mouth now merely swishes silently out through a hole in his neck; he knows how much he has lost. The speechless person with aphasia resulting from a stroke or automobile accident knows but he cannot tell us. In certain ancient cultures the tearing out of a victim's tongue was the ultimate punishment, worse than death itself. It is through the use of speech and language that we live together, work, earn our livings, win our mates, and find our meanings in the pinpoint of time and space that we inhabit. Yet few of us ever give our speech more than casual attention; few of us ever view it as the most important instrument we will ever learn to manipulate.

It seems almost incredible that so important a skill as speaking should receive so little attention or training. Even in teaching a baby to talk, the usual pedagogy is so poor that were we taught to read by the same type of procedure, we would be a nation of illiterates. We provide the wrong models often at the wrong times. We overwhelm the baby with demands, commands, and requests for words and phrases for which he has little need at the moment. Too often we talk to him incessantly in compound complex sentences, hiding the sounds of speech in words hidden in phrases hidden in paragraphs of meaningless utterance, while we tickle his ribs and jounce him in the air. It is better when we patiently play "patty-cake," accompanying speech with gesture, or label his eyes and ears and toes, or tell him simply what he is doing or seeing. Fortunately, most children learn to speak a few words and sentences despite this pedagogy, and when they do, we abruptly stop all our efforts to teach them anything else about the uses and functions of this new power they have acquired. From then on, they are on their own to get by themselves, catch-as-catch-can, all the rest of their speaking skills. Thereafter there is an occasional correction of a mispronunciation, the providing of a missing word, or a rare demand to speak up or speak clearly. That is about all the training they get until they take a speech class in high school or in college. Our question is: Is this enough? The human race has presented us with a precious tool that can do incredible things, one with tremendous potential. Shouldn't we learn how to exploit that potential?

If we are to learn the use of any tool, we must examine it. Yet when that tool is our speech, we somehow recoil from confronting it, perhaps because it mirrors the self. We listen to our own recordings with fearful reluctance or with morbid fascination or denial. When asked to display our speech before a group of listeners, we dread the judgments in their eyes. What speech teacher, when he has been introduced as such, has not found a new acquaintance become stiff-tongued and falteringly careful? We want to talk as we walk, without self-directed attention. We want to talk as we breathe, with no awareness of the process. Listen to what I say, not to how I say it, is our implicit demand. We recognize these objections as valid descriptions of feelings, but we do not believe that one becomes an expert golfer by merely observing the ball after it has been hit. Some scrutiny of what happens as we speak may be, similarly, a prerequisite to improvement in speaking. Fortunately, in this book we will necessarily be speaking about speech in somewhat general terms, and the personal application of what we say may be made by the reader to himself in privacy. But we reject completely the assumption that it is unwise to explore why we speak and how we speak. How else will we ever be able to learn to exploit all the potentials of the gift that enabled man to emerge from the cave, conquer the earth, and reach for the stars?

When we do take a long hard look at speech we see that it possesses three immediately obvious features: the *motoric*, the *acoustic*, and the *symbolic*. It consists of movements and sounds and meanings. It also serves a variety of functions. In the remaining chapters of this text we shall discuss some of these functions in some detail, dealing with them in terms of emotional speech, egocentric speech, communicative speech, speech for control, and speech as the tool of thought. Here we will confine ourselves to the three basic features of speech, not its functions.

Motoric Speech

Many volumes larger than this one would be required to describe the marvelous machinery that produces speech. The first of these would describe the nervous system and how it functions. It would contain diagrams of the surface layer of your brain (the cortex) showing the major lobes: occipital (primarily for vision), temporal (primarily for hearing), parietal (primarily for sensory discriminations of size, shape, and posture), and frontal (for initiating muscular movements and for thinking). It would show that your brain is twinned, with duplicate hemispheres on each side, though the left hemisphere apparently is of major importance in speech. Just this surface layer of the brain, the cortex, carries an incredibly complex network of almost ten billion nerve cells. Despite the devoted lives of many scientists, our knowledge of its functioning still has many gaps. But in that volume there would also be some exciting accounts of their discoveries. You would read how surgeons such as Penfield(1) were able to map the motor and sensory areas by stimulating spots on the brain with an electrode to make a group of muscles twitch or to cause a sensation to be reported by their epileptic subjects who remained conscious throughout the experiment. You might find accounts, reading almost like horror stories, of tumors or traumatic injuries or of the deliberate sectioning of the frontal lobes and of what happened to the speech and language and personalities of these patients. You would learn that the experimenter, by turning on a little current in one place, could produce either complete stoppage of speech or repetitive speech similar to stuttering, and that by switching the electrode to another place he could evoke hallucinations or recreate memories. You would also learn that your brain beats constantly with rhythmic waves of electrical potential sweeping across the cortex, that these brain waves can be altered or driven by different stimuli including speech, and that the sleeping state and conscious thinking affect them differently. You would become entangled in theory and speculation, but you would surely become aware of the fact that this simple business of talking is a miracle of the utmost complexity.

If you read on, you would find that leading downward from the motor areas of the cortex (the surface layer of the brain) toward the actual machinery of speech (the lips, tongue, vocal cords, and chest muscles) are cables containing many bundles of nerve fibers. One of the most important of these cables is called the *pyramidal tract*. Its nerve fibers descend downward from the fifth layer of the cortex through the bulb of your midbrain. Then they cross over to the other side and go down to their junction with the nerves in the spinal cord that run outward to some of the muscles that produce speech. This is the cable that carries the messages we use to control the conscious and voluntary activities of the body. When it is injured, control is lost; muscles become overtense, spastic, and clumsily uncoordinated. This pathway for the nervous impulses must be intact for all the coordinated skills such as writing, typing, playing a musical instrument, or speaking. It was the last to develop in the course of evolution and is the last to mature in the baby. The nerve impulses that run down this cable inhibit random movements and organize purposeful ones. Just saying the one word "Nuts!" represents a veritable symphony of nervous impulses arising in the brain stuff and flowing downward to the muscles.

The second major channel down which nerve impulses flow to your speech machinery is called the *extrapyramidal tract*. These impulses go downward, again from the cortex, are mixed and modified by other controlling impulses from the midbrain (the thalamus, globus pallidus, caudate nucleus, and so forth), and then join the terminals of the nerves that run outward to the muscles used in speech.

Most of the muscles used in speaking are arranged in sets so that they oppose each other. As one set contracts, its opposing set of antagonistic muscles relaxes progressively. The mere act of opening your mouth to say "Ah" requires an incredibly balanced action of such opposing sets of muscles. Nerve impulses descending down this extrapyramidal channel regulate such functions as the pitch of your voice, the provision of sufficient air for speech, and the smooth fluency of utterance, among other things.

The third major nerve cable is the *cerebellar motor pathway*. Behind the midbrain and below the cortex is a spherical mass of brain tissue, the cerebellum. The cerebellum has been called the hind brain or bird brain. We are all bird-brained creatures—bird-brained and mammal-brained and, most important of all, man-brained. Impulses from the cerebellum set the muscles of speech in a state of readiness to contract, coordinate breathing with the movements of the lips and tongue, and monitor the flow of speech. When the cerebellum is hurt by tumor or disease, speech becomes distorted and uncoordinated. Such speakers sound horribly drunk.

We have summarized briefly the main system that energizes the muscles used in speech production, but we cannot conclude our discussion without at least some passing reference to the back flow of nervous impulses that goes upward from those muscles to the brain. The nervous system is like a pair of escalators—one descending, the other ascending. Nervous impulses not only go downward from the brain to the muscles; they also ascend. Without this upward feedback, all coordinations would become disrupted. In a recent experiment by Ringel, (2) when the mouth cavity was deeply anesthetized, the speaker immediately began to make errors in his speech, to slur and distort his sounds, and to have breaks in his fluency. All of us who have ever gone to the dentist have experienced this in a mild degree. We need this *feedback* from the structures used in speaking if we are to speak precisely, indeed if we are to speak at all.

Another source of feedback control, of course, is the ear. The congenitally deaf never learn to speak completely normally even after intensive tutoring, and the person who becomes completely deafened later in life usually finds that his speech begins to decay in clarity. Sounds become slurred and vocal inflections become abnormal; the deafened person may alternately speak too softly or blast his utterance too loudly. He lacks the necessary feedback.

The speech scientists have invented a curious machine called the *delayed auditory feedback apparatus* which slows the self-hearing of the speaker by a fifth of a second. Were you to speak into this infernal machine, you would find yourself stuttering, slurring, speaking in an odd voice, or even thinking incoherently. And all that has happened is that you are hearing your own speech fed back to your brain a fifth of a second after it should be. This curious experience reveals a most important fact. Our speech is operated by automation, by a servo-system. It is run by a system of unconscious automatic controls, as a furnace is controlled by a thermostat or an airplane by an automatic pilot. Up from the muscles and the ear, there flows to the brain a continuous current of information which is used to integrate the outflow of utterance.

All we have done here is to skim over the huge mass of information we possess about the way our nervous system functions in speech. Surely, no one who contemplates the intricacies of this marvelous system can ever fail to appreciate the miracle of speaking.

The Speaking Machinery

Volume II of the series of texts that describe the process of speaking would have at least three sections, one on *respiration* or breathing, one on *phonation* or the production of voice, and the third on *articulation* or the production of the consonants and vowels. Essentially it would describe the basic apparatus used in speech production, name the muscles, bones, and cartilages, and show how they work. In abstracting this material we will confine ourselves to only the major core of information.

The breathing apparatus, for example, operates much like the Scottish bagpipes. The lung bags lie in the thorax (the chest), and when your ribs are raised or the dome-shaped floor of your chest cavity (the diaphragm) is lowered, air is sucked into them via the mouth, nose, and windpipe as the chest cavity expands. When the muscles that raise the ribs or lower the floor relax or are forcibly opposed by other muscles such as those encasing the abdomen, the thorax collapses and the air is forced out and upward to create the necessary air pressure that sets the closed vocal folds vibrating.

> At one time, speech and singing teachers used to train their students to take a deep breath, fix the expanded chest, and then contract the abdomen forcibly because they thought that this was the most efficient way of producing voice. They said that this was the natural way to breathe because babies breathed this way. But our scientists have shown that the ribs of babies run horizontally, rather than slantwise as in the adult, and so they naturally show more abdominal breathing than we do.

Our present research indicates that there is no one proper way of breathing for speech, that some superior speakers use more thoracic breathing and others more abdominal, that the most important thing is merely to take in enough breath and to use it economically. This does not mean at all that we should take a deep inspiration before beginning to talk; the inhalation for ordinary speech should not be any greater than in silent breathing—though it will be a bit quicker as shown in Figure 1. The important thing is to control the exhalation smoothly. Some speakers, especially when under stress, develop bad habits of inhaling too deeply, then expelling much of this air, and then speaking with strain on the residual air that remains. Others gasp, showing what is called *"staircase" breathing* or *air wastages.* When these are merely the result of emotion or poor body postures, the cure is adaptation or adjustment; when they become habitual, they must be brought to consciousness so that they can be rejected. Usually most of us, even under great stress, breathe adequately enough to produce strong voice.

How We Produce Sound

Another section of Volume II of the series would discuss the mechanism of phonation. It would describe the three major cartilages of the larynx: the foundation cartilage that looks like a signet ring, called the *cricoid;* the butterfly-shaped *thyroid* to which the front ends of the vocal folds are attached; and the two little *arytenoids* that bring together the rear ends of those vocal folds so that they can be set into vibration. The vocal folds themselves are more like muscular lips than like cords, and their edges are thin and

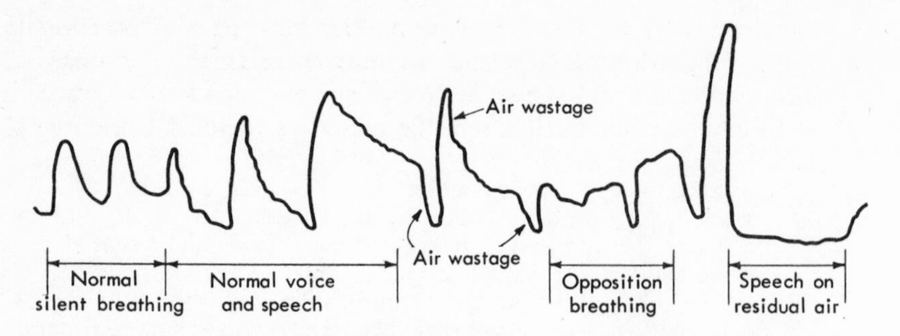

FIGURE 1. *Breathing Abnormalities.* (From C. Van Riper, *Speech Correction: Principles and Methods,* 4th ed. Englewood Cliffs, N.J.: Prentice-Hall, Inc., 1963, p. 169).

elastic. As the air pressure beneath them builds up, they are finally blown apart and set into rhythmic vibration, thus creating sound. By changing their tension, changes in pitch and loudness can be produced. Normally we time the closure of the vocal folds so that it coincides with the breath pulse from the lungs. Those speakers who close their vocal folds partially or a little too late tend to show husky or breathy voices like "Hot-breath Harriet." Those who close the vocal folds too early and hold them too tightly together so that excessive air pressure is required to blow them apart (the "hard attack") often show strained, harsh voices and may even develop the little wart-like bumps on the folds that are called vocal nodules. These can interfere greatly with phonation and can even produce a loss of voice. Most of us lose our voices only when laryngitis causes the folds to become inflamed and thickened so that they vibrate with difficulty, or when we abuse them by straining in the presence of too much noise. It is sensible vocal hygiene at such times to talk little and to talk softly.

The tone produced by the vocal folds themselves is not a very pleasant sound. Experiments have been performed in which the larynx of a cadaver has been removed and hooked up to a tank of air under pressure. By exerting force to tighten the vocal folds, sounds have been produced but they are more squawks than tones, much like the sound produced by the isolated mouthpiece of a trumpet. In the living person, the vocal cords have above them the tubes and cavities of the throat, mouth, and nose, and these act as resonating horns to produce not squawks but tones. The beauty of the human voice could never be achieved without these resonators. Many of us never learn to use these resonators with the skill necessary for the production of a voice as pleasant and efficient as it might be. We mute the opening by talking through lips too close together; we strain the muscular walls of the resonators; we emit too much of the sound nasally. Squeezing the walls of the throat with the muscles produces harshness of tone.

The final section of Volume II would describe the articulators, the tongue, jaw, lips, and soft palate. These work in wondrous ways to produce the consonants and vowels. We have looked through a plastic window in the cheek of a person who had had that section removed because of cancer, and we have witnessed slow motion X-ray movies of healthy tongues and palates that had been painted with barium paste. The motion of the tongue is pure poetry even in the utterance of such a prosaic test sentence as "The quick brown fox jumped over the lazy dog." It moves with a sinuous grace, flowing from contour to contour. We watch a person say *two*. The jaws part and the soft palate descends as the person takes a breath, then the palate smoothly rises to block off the rear passageway to the nasal cavities. Then the tongue flows upward and forward, brushing the inner part of the upper gum, gracefully shifts rearward to an upraised posture, then down again. Again we marvel at the incredible coordination required for the production of just a tiny syllable, remembering that this is the work not of single muscles but of twins, for all the muscles used in speech are paired. Even the tongue, beneath its covering, is a complicated matrix of paired muscles. How do we ever learn to talk?

Speech as Sound: The Acoustic Aspect

No instrument is more versatile than the human voice. When we survey the diversity of sounds used in the thousands of languages and dialects that resound in this earthly Tower of Babel, we cannot help but be amazed. In Africa, there are tribes that communicate with a few vowels interspersed with mouth clicks and sucking noises almost indescribable in their variety. These sounds can be found elsewhere only in the little noises and gurglings of any human baby who, after all, does not yet know if he will grow up to be an American or a Hottentot and so must practice all the sounds. In Asia, we hear the singsong of the Chinese tonal languages. In the Canary Islands, people even use a whistle language to carry their meanings from mountain top to valley. The French language sounds nasal, except to the Frenchman; the German, gutteral and explosive except to the German. The Americans sense British speech as being overly clipped and staccato; the English feel that we speak harshly, nasally, and very sloppily. The human instrument for speech is capable of many tones and noises.

Oddly enough, it is very difficult for us to listen to or to hear objectively the speech sounds we produce. We use our ears primarily to hear our thoughts—and the thoughts of others. Radio announcers often cup their hands to their ears, altering the sound field about their heads to which they have become overly adapted, in order to know how they sound. Over and over again they listen to their tape recordings in order to improve. Most of us find this self-listening not only very difficult but somehow threatening. "Ouch!" we cry. "Is this how I sound to others? Must be a poor recording device." Yet other voices on the same tape sound quite familiar and true.

Let us, then, examine the acoustic stuff of which our speech is composed. We find, first of all, that it consists of tones, noises, and bits of silence, all combined in specific sequences to carry specific meanings. All the vowels are tonal and each vowel is a homogenized blending of many component tones called *formants*. C. F. Hockett, the linguist, has compared their composition to unboiled Easter eggs of various sizes and colors, carried on a continuous belt through a wringer, smashed and blended together to make a complex sound. Oddly enough the analogy is fairly accurate. Even scholars can get poetic at times.

> You may have learned in grade school that we have only six vowels—"*a, e, i, o, u,* and sometimes *y.*" Actually we have many more in spoken English. *In just this one short sentence you should be able to find over ten different vowels and at least two diphthongs.* All the vowels and diphthongs in English are included except the vowel "ah" as in *father*, and the diphthong "oy" as in *boy*. (Diphthongs are blends of two sequential vowels as in *ouch, boy,* and *eye.*) It is almost impossible to represent many of the sounds by using the symbols of our conventional alphabet; therefore, special phonetic alphabets have been invented in which each symbol stands for only one sound or phoneme.

Although, as the researcher Elbert R. Moses(3) once discovered, no one says the same sound always in the same way on the same day, the variations are minor and not significant so far as the meaning is concerned. We can understand people who use dialects other than ours. In this country there appear to be three major dialects, the General American spoken by more than a hundred million of us, and the Eastern and Southern by the rest. A few slightly different vowels are found in the latter two, variants of the *a* sound as in *cat* or the *o* sound as in *hot*. They say these and the *r* sounds differently than the majority of Americans. In some forms of Southern speech, triphthongs (sequences of three vowels blended together) are to be heard. And there are other differences. Again, within each of these major dialectal divisions much individual variation occurs, permitting skilled phoneticians to locate a person's origin by the way he speaks.

> Although all of us have been speaking for years, it is surprising how little most of us really know about the sounds we use. What sound is produced by whispering a *v*? (The *f*.) How do you shape your tongue to produce an *r*? (You use a double, camelback-shaped contour.) What two vowels combine to produce the vowel "i" as in the word *eye*? (Ah plus ih [ɑɪ] or [aɪ].) What sound has a high-pitched sort of whistle in it? (The *s*.) If you hold your nose and say "maybe" swiftly, what word comes out? (Baby.) What three sounds are made by putting the back of your tongue against your soft palate? (The *k*, *g*, and *ng* sounds.) From where does the little click come that begins the word "hour"? (From the vocal folds.)

Consonants are those speech noises we use to initiate or to interrupt the flow of vowel tone. Some of them, the *plosives*, are popping sounds, which are produced by damming up the airstream behind the tongue or lips, then releasing it with tiny puffs of air. Such sounds as *t*, *d*, *k*, *g*, *p*, and *b* are plosives. Other consonant noises called *fricatives* are made by squeezing the channels through which the air or sound is emitted. The *s*, *z*, *sh*, *zh*, *f*, *v*, and *th* sounds belong to this group. And there are a few sounds, the *affricates*, which combine the characteristics of both plosives and fricatives. The *ch* and *j* sounds are affricates. You can produce, for example, a good *ch* by combining a *t* (plosive) with an *sh* (fricative). Try alternating the words *it* and *she* swiftly. You will inevitably find yourself saying "itchy." We also have a few *glide* sounds in English, such as the *w* and the *y*, which are almost impossible to make in isolation because their essential noises are made by the mouth in motion, the *w* being produced by shifting from the posture of the vowel *oo* to that of the vowel that follows as in the words *way* or *we*. Three of our consonants are nasals, the *m*, *n*, and *ng*. To produce these, we lower the soft palate—the back door to the nose—and the sound reverberates in the nasal cavities. By lightly touching the side of your nose while making these sounds, you can feel the vibration. Finally we have two sounds, the *l* and the *r*, which are fricative when they start a syllable, as in the words *love* and *red*, but which are also tonal and vowel-like, acting as vowels in such words as *bottle* or *bird*. They have been called *semivowels*.

One curious feature we discover when we begin to look at these consonants which we have been producing so automatically for so long is that many of them are twins, and a few are even triplets. The *t* and *d* sounds, for example, are made almost identically except for the fact that the *d* is produced with vocal-fold vibration (sonant), whereas the *t* is whispered (surd). There are many of these pairs; the *p* and *b*, the *k* and *g*, the *s* and *z*, and others. We also have a few sets of triplet sounds which are articulated very similarly, but in which one is voiced and nasal, one is merely voiced, and the third whispered. The *n*, *d*, and *t* comprise such a trio, and perhaps you can discover another set of triplets for yourself. In our own mouths there are many discoveries to be made.

When these consonants are scrutinized closely we also note that they vary in pitch and duration. The *s* and *sh* sounds, for example, are both sibilants (sounds with hissing or whistle noises), but the hiss is higher in pitch for the *s* than it is for the *sh*. In the *f* and the *th*, the pitch difference is present but smaller—which is why so many children, not hearing the distinction, tend to say *fink* for *think* and *free* for *three*. Some continue to lisp all their lives. When we consider the plosives (the popping sounds such as *p*, *t*, *d*, or *g*) we find that they are much shorter in duration just because they do explode. The plosives are shorter than the affricates and these shorter than the fricatives and these in turn than the vowels. Note the difference in duration of the following: *t*, *ch*, *sh*, *ah*. The human ear must scan all these minute differences in order to decide the subtleties of meanings. Again we marvel at the sensitivity of our discriminations. Truly we are fearfully and wonderfully made.

It might be said that in speaking we play the role of an orchestra conductor. Each sound may be viewed as being produced by a different instrument; each vowel by a different horn. Some of the horns, such as those used for the *oo* and *oh*, have small flared openings; others, such as that for the *ah*, have a big opening that is not flared. The mouth tube assumes a different shape for each

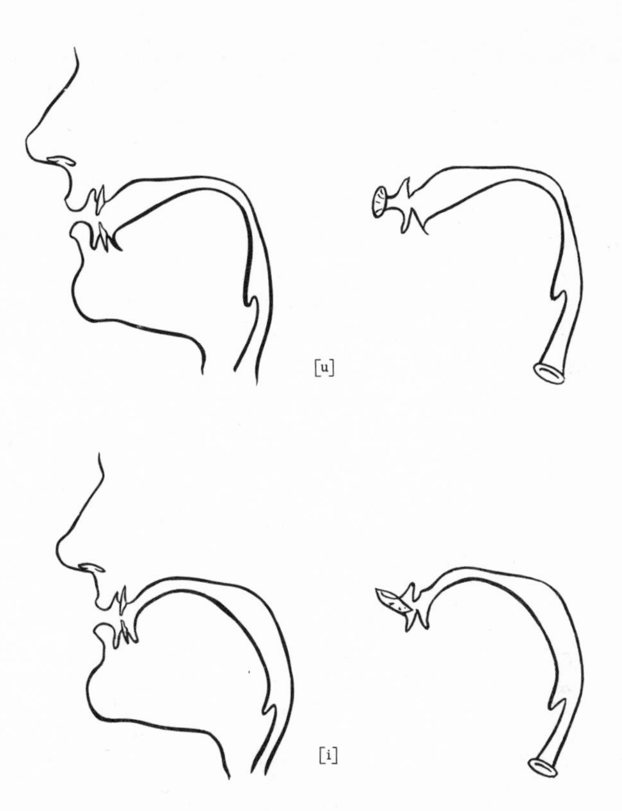

FIGURE 2. *Resonating Cavities for Two Vowels.*

vowel, and this enables it to amplify a distinctive set of overtones. But an orchestra needs percussion instruments as well as horns, and by using the tongue and lips we produce the punctuating beats of the plosive sounds and the swish of the fricatives. Imagine the complicated symphonic score that would be needed to program a sentence such as this one.

We must also remember that the instruments of our speech orchestra also produce melody, with changes of pitch and loudness in the utterance of different meanings. We are not Johnny-one-notes; we ask questions; we make statements; we protest; we emphasize; and with each variation, changes in pitch and loudness are required. The pitch is largely determined by the rate at which the vocal folds vibrate, and this in turn by their length and tension. Loudness variations are caused partly by how far the vocal folds are blown apart and partly by how efficiently we resonate. Skilled speakers, in full command of their speech instruments, can project their voices to fill huge halls even without a microphone. They know how to shape their mouth horns, how to prolong their vowels, and they know how to make the speech noises, the consonants, so that they will "carry." Few of us ever experiment enough to discover these skills or to learn to conduct our speech orchestra with either art or precision.

Any musical composition has symbols for pauses in its score; so must speech. Not only do the combinations of tones and noises carry meanings; so also do the bits of silence. We punctuate with pauses. We group our thoughts and indicate their patterning with little moments of silence. For example, say this series of words aloud; woman, without, her, man, would, be, a, beast. By inserting bits of silence in different places you could have the words mean either: "Woman! Without her, man would be a beast," or "Woman, without her man, would be a beast." Gaps as well as sounds can have significance.

Speech as Symbol: The Linguistic Factor

Magpies, crows, parrots, and mynah birds have been taught to talk. We have even heard a recording of a "talking dog" who growled something resembling the word "hamburger." These creatures have the sounds of speech but not the symbols. At best, they are but recording machines that can emit only the sounds that have been put into them. Their songs once learned are fixed. They do not create. Thus their utterances are without meanings, in the human sense. Never can the mynah change the order of those words or substitute a synonym. Polly may want a cracker, but the bird is not asking for one even when it says the sentence. These are mocking birds, not human beings.

We have taught several birds and many children to speak. Up to a certain point the process is the same. We create a pleasant, nonfrightening situation; then, when the baby or bird is making a series of repetitive sounds, we interrupt by producing the same sound, whereupon the bird or baby responds by continuing. Thus, their responses follow ours and are of the same form, almost as though imitation had occurred. We immediately reward the bird by food or drink and the baby by either of these or by loving care and fondling. After enough of this has occurred, we stimulate them with a simple word or phrase which occasionally they then repeat, often distortedly at first. Gradually the utterance of the bird or baby comes to approximate our own, if the reinforcement has been programmed appropriately and efficiently. But it is at this point that the human being demonstrates his god-stuff. While both the baby and the bird may be saying "Mama," only the baby uses the word when she appears and uses it to call her, and soon he seeks another word for the other giants that surround him. If these people name themselves "Daddy" and "Sue," the child soon learns their labels. The smooth, round, red object becomes a "ball," because others have used that word when it was being seen, felt, or thrown. The bird's word is at best only an expression of an internal state, similar to the purring of a contented kitten. The baby's word becomes a symbol, a representation. The bird's word is a cry, the baby's word is a designation. The human being, unlike other creatures, is able to refer, to signify, to make meaningful sounds.

That a baby ever learns to talk at all is almost incredible to the person who understands the nature of the task. We have already seen the complexity of the coordinations and sounds which he must master. But when we consider the problems encountered in being able to use meaningful language, we can hardly believe that any ordinary mortal could solve them. Not only must he master the simple names of the objects that surround him and know their referents, he must also learn the intricate laws of the language—laws that linguistic scholars are still exploring. There are hundreds of unwritten, unspoken rules to discover and remember and use. Each language has its own structure, and those who use it must conform. Anyone who has had to master a second language in adulthood knows how difficult this achievement is. Although learning a vocabulary is hard enough, this is the simplest of all the skills required. It is the phrasing, the construction of sentences, and the syntax that give the most trouble. Yet little children learn these things and do so unthinkingly and easily.

Once again, let us try to make clear the immense achievement that speaking represents. Speech consists of a learned set of conventional sound-signs governed by a set of operational rules that determine how they may be combined. Basic elements in this code are the *phonemes* (the distinctive speech sounds).

Perhaps some illustration may be helpful here. We can make our *s* sounds in slightly different ways and still be understood, even when we are a bit intoxicated or are first fitted with false teeth. Indeed, we normally use a slightly different *s* sound in the word *see* than we do in the word *sue*. If you say these two words aloud, you will notice that the first *s* is higher in pitch than the second. The *s* therefore represents, not a completely single sound but a family of very similar sounds whose differences make no difference in the meaning. This is what is meant by a phoneme. It is a family of very similar sounds whose differences have no significance.

In each language the various phonemes can be combined only in certain ways to form meaningful words. For example, English has no word that begins with an *ng* sound, although many African languages do. A child or a foreigner must learn these phonemic rules as well as master the sounds of English and the meanings of the words.

Speaking also requires the mastery of an immense number of *morphemes*. A morpheme is the shortest linguistic unit that possesses meaning. We are now talking about meanings, not just sounds. Morphemes are composed of phonemes, but the sounds must make sense. The phoneme *n* makes no sense and has no meaning no matter how long you prolong or repeat it. But when it is combined with the phonemes *o* and *z* in different ways, it can contribute to the creation of the three morphemes: *nose*, *owns*, and *zone*. Words can contain more than one morpheme, however. The word *boy* is one morpheme; the word *boy's* has two morphemes, since the *'s* indicates the meaning of possession. The *sh* in the word *shoe* is a phoneme only. It must be joined with the phoneme *oo* (spelled *oe* here) in order to make the morpheme meaning footwear. But "Sh!" alone, as a command to be quiet, is a phoneme and, because it has a specific meaning, is a morpheme, too. The word *boys* also has two morphemes in it, one indicating the male child and the other the fact of the plural. If this sounds complicated, remember that every child must learn hundreds of these hidden rules of language if he is to communicate at all. Speaking is a very complex business.

Finally, to speak a language means that one must discover and follow the rules of *syntax*, learning the principles that govern the ways in which words can be arranged together in meaningful groupings. Children soon learn that one-morpheme utterances such as "Mama" or "Down!" are not enough; they are too limited. They need to learn how to join words together, and that means learning certain rules of syntax. We cannot say, "Throw the cow over the fence some hay," without sounding strange or foreign.

We who have spoken so much for so long find it very difficult to appreciate the immense achievement which speaking represents. It seems so easy. Even tiny children learn to do it. But if we take a long look backward to view the slow process of evolution and then another look forward into the mist of the future, we cannot help but recognize the exciting fact that man has broken free from the tyranny of biological mutation through the invention of speech and language. The dream of a superman no longer needs to depend upon structural chance and change, upon the occurence of a new species that will be better adapted to environment than we are. Through the invention of symbols, verbal and mathematical, we have been able to create our own environment on land, beneath the seas, and even in outer space. We can store the wisdom gathered by our wisest men over the course of centuries, each new generation being able to build upon the contributions of its predecessors.

But may we not hope for even more? The accumulation of knowledge is not enough if we cannot learn to use it for better purposes than self-destruction. May we not hope that man can learn to conquer himself, can really exploit the potential of his ten billion brain cells? The incredible advances in science show what the exploitation of mathematical symbols can do for us. If only we could learn to do the same with our verbal symbols, would we not take the great leap forward? The ancient Greeks created their gods, their mythical supermen, in their own idealized image. Our own future race of supermen may look little different than we, but they will be able to use their language symbols in ways which we can now discern only dimly. We may hope that their young will be skillfully trained to speak, rather than merely encouraged to do so, and that the training will be long and complex—but attractive. Through programmed language learning they will discover how to encode experience, retrieve it, and predict it. They will be trained to know themselves by verbal means and to find the exploration comfortable and enticing, not terrifying as it is to those of us who fear ourselves. There will be little insanity, less crime, and no poverty. Communication will be more exact and without compulsive distortion. These supermen of the future will find thinking easy rather than difficult. They will call forth the emotions appropriate to the task at hand instead of being lashed and controlled by inappropriate ones that take command. People will be able to live together and work together and share together the fruits of their creativity. Yes, this is an old dream from which many generations have awakened only to have their energies wasted on the evil reality about them. But may we remember that as yet we have never learned to exploit the incredible potential inherent in our ability to symbolize. We use only a fraction of the powers of speech and language. We are still unskilled and primitive. We are still that ape that uses a flute to scratch himself. Our descendants of the far future will use their language to conquer themselves, as we have used ours to conquer the earth. The fact that man has learned to talk at all, in view of the incredible complexity of the task, gives us hope that this vision will someday be reality.

In this text we hope to describe the dim beginnings of the evolutionary process, for the needs of the future are already with us. We will attempt to describe how we currently use our speech to define ourselves, to express and control our emotions, to live socially together, to communicate information and demands, and to think. In the forthcoming chapters we will doubtless demonstrate how crudely we fumble with this magical key that will one day unlock the door to man's future, but we hope to show that even now we have made a beginning.

2 Speech as Emotional Expression

More than half of all the hospital beds in this country are filled with patients having severe emotional problems. A miserable statistic indicates that one person in every five will undergo some type of mental illness before he dies. Only an incurable optimist such as Voltaire's Pangloss could insist (even after he lost one buttock) that this is the best of all possible worlds. Our lives are not easy ones. We run a hazardous gauntlet from birth to death, and many blows rain down upon us. Competitive, aggressive, suspicious, our culture demands much of its frail membership. All of us must expect failures, penalties, and frustrations. All of us will often experience anxiety, guilt, and hostility, those evil acids that eat their containers. The picture, of course, is not as dark as it seems, for life holds good moments too, and they can form a majority if we learn to live healthy emotional lives.

Emotions color most of our experiences, though, like sound itself, they range in intensity from below the threshold of awareness to levels that can be catastrophic. At one time, psychologists felt that thought and emotion were separate identities; now we know that they are closely conjoined, though certain experiences are more highly saturated by emotion than others. The perception that one plus one equals two as in mathematics, for example, has less emotional upheaval in it than the perception that one plus one equals one, as in mating. Since the melody of our lives must be played to the accompaniment of pleasant or unpleasant feelings, we must somehow learn to fit them into our living patterns so they harmonize rather than disrupt with discord. This task is perhaps the greatest challenge still facing man. He has shown thus far that he can conquer almost everything except himself. Yet we know that this too is possible.

Every generation, indeed every community, produces some individuals who seem to have learned how to live graciously. Somehow they have managed to run the gauntlet successfully. We tend to attribute their achievement to luck, perhaps, but man's history holds thousands of noted persons who achieved serenity and fulfillment despite lives filled with tragedy. How many others, unknown and unsung, have done as well? We know not, but we have the faith that there have been millions more. How did they learn to live the good life? How did they learn to live in harmony with themselves and their surroundings? Doubtless, some of them found the answers in religion, some in helping others, many in conquering a wilderness, others in creating a happy household, a few in making symphonies, a multitude hoeing a garden. Somehow, they learned to fulfill their potentials, to find strength from their pleasant emotional experiences and to survive their unpleasant ones without self-destruction.

Language and Emotion

It is amazing to discover how crucial a role our speech plays in the tragi-comedy of life. Consider just the concept of failure. It is through words that we set our goals, define our aspirations, evaluate our performances. The ache of defeat may merely reflect the fact that we have verbalized to ourselves demands which were completely unrealistic. We may have accepted the exorbitant demands of others to achieve the unwanted or the impossible. One of our students told us a sad tale just before he flunked out of the university in the final semester of his senior year.

> Six words have wrecked my life. I've heard them ever since I was a baby. I've heard them thousands of times. 'You're going to be a doctor,' my parents told me over and over. My folks never had much of an education, but both of them worked terribly hard ever since I was born to save enough to put me through medical school. My dad moonlighted for years, working one job in the day and another at night, saving money, always saving so I could be

a doctor. I guess it was because my older brother died before I was born because he couldn't get the proper medical attention. Anyway, that was what they said I was going to be, and for years I thought so too. I studied hard even in the science courses I hated. I've always been more interested in art and music and the theater but I had to be a doctor; I had to be a doctor. I had to take chemistry and biology and anatomy. Had to cut up worms, then cats, then cadavers. Always hurt to do it. Can't stand pain or suffering. I'd make a hell of a doctor. These six little words are eighty feet tall and weigh eighty tons and I don't know how much longer I can bear them.

Psychologists tell us that the most satisfying way to live is to set our aspiration levels just far enough above our performance levels so that occasionally or eventually they can be attained, and to continuously revise our verbal statements of goals and evaluations in terms of actual achievement. How many of our moments of anxiety, depression, guilt, or self-hatred come from the failure to verbalize our goals realistically or to evaluate our achievements honestly? Some of us even refuse our basic responsibility for doing either, passively accepting what others tell us to do or be. It is tragic that our educational system devotes so little of its time to teaching us the powers for good or evil that speech possesses. Surely someday this will be changed.

Time Binding

Many of our miseries are due to the language we use in describing ourselves. These self-referring adjectives can be poisonous. "I'm lazy." "I'm just not very bright." "I'm unattractive." "I'm helpless." "I'm no good." The moment we say these things we commit ourselves to a distorted identity. We mistake the verbalization for the verity. All of us are lazy occasionally—and indeed usually—when somebody else sets up goals which do not appeal to our needs. All of us have moments of stupidity; all of us can be very unattractive at times. Not one of us can always be good, whatever that means, all the time. Whenever we find ourselves using this sort of emotionally toned evaluative speech, we should stop abruptly and doubt and test the reality. We should first of all examine the real evidence behind the adjective and then *date* that evidence in time. By this we mean that behavior is time-bound. It is a matter of the moment. Under such and such circumstances, and at such and such a time, you showed a bit of behavior which might be labeled as "lazy," or "stupid," or something else. And that moment already has passed; it is an infinitesimal part of your history; it need not set your course and shape your entire future. Tragically, this simple principle of mental health seems unknown to most of us. We do not realize that the magic of speech can also be black magic, that the things we say about ourselves possess incredible power to determine what we may become.

Depression is full of this disparaging self-talk. The same old sentences reverberate in our skulls like nagging tunes. They are a continuous circle of elephants draped in black, holding each other's tails, marching to the dirge of our self-condemnation or self-pity. That dirge always has a lyric to its mournful melody, and the words of that lyric are mainly miserable adjectives about ourselves, words that are untrue because they are not dated.

Words and Reality

Many emotional problems arise because we confuse words with things. Suzuki, a follower of Zen Buddhism, says, "Words are words and no more. When words cease to correspond with facts it is time for us to part with words and return to facts."(1) Nevertheless, it is difficult for us to realize that words are intrinsically only little puffs of sound or clusters of letters on a page. They are useful only insofar as they represent reality. Alas, they often misrepresent.

> Jonathan Swift once wrote: "It was a bold man that first ate an oyster." It was also a brave man that first ate a tomato. Until the beginning of this century, tomatoes, or love-apples as they were called, were considered poisonous. Generation after generation had passed the word along: "Love-apples are poisonous."

We have already discussed the difficulties we get into when we talk about ourselves in words that fail to represent reality. We must also remember that the words other people use to describe us may be as distorted as our own. Much of our misery comes from the words other people have used to label us. We accept their verbal caricature as the truth and build our lives on their falsities. These adjectives are so powerful in shaping our existence that many of us become slaves, shackled to the tyranny of opinion. We perform more badly than we need to in situations where others are judging us. The student speaker quakes and often becomes tongue-tied before a new audience. The teenager kills himself in his car to escape the epithet of "chicken." We live beyond our means. We pretend to be that which we are not. How many anxieties stem from the miserable anticipation of the labels which others might possibly bestow upon us? Perhaps, someday we will be taught, from the cradle and throughout our entire education, to examine these adjectives and to accept them with caution. Each one of them needs to be scrutinized in terms of the *when, where,* and *why* of the underlying evidence. Must we grow up to be as vulnerable as the child in the first year of school, crying because some other little child has called him "Kindergarten baby, slopped in the gravy"? Perhaps we must learn to respond, as he should, with a sophisticated form of the "Sticks and stones will break my bones, but names will never hurt me." Names can hurt—but only if they are accepted uncritically.

The Allness Error

Emotionally toned speech consists of statements as well as single epithets. They too can hurt, but more often they mislead, which is even worse. One of the major language errors is that of faulty generalization. It's so easy to use the word "all" and then to believe the statement which it introduces. For example, many of our fears and phobias are due to this misuse of language. "I'm afraid of snakes" may be a reasonably accurate commentary on our *feelings* that snakes are poisonous or that they wiggle or that they are slimy. But only a rare handful of all the hundreds of species of snakes are poisonous, and none of them are slimy; they feel like sandpaper. As for wiggling, well there's always the hula dancer! Perhaps the real reason lies in none of these. You fear snakes because your mother or your older brother told you they feared them and because they planted into the furrows of your brain the statement that all snakes are creatures to be feared. The basic error lies in the concept that the general semanticists call "allness." All snakes are not to be feared. Even the poisonous rattlers or cobras should not have the power to cause you to recoil or run if they are secured behind the glass barrier in the zoo. We need to use our language so that it does not generalize too widely, so that we index our experiences specifically. Not all snakes, nor any snake in all circumstances, should cause fear.

Although snake fears present little problem for most of us, we have plenty of others that do bedevil our lives. Many of them are just as groundless. The energy and time we spend in worrying could be better spent in examining the validity of the statements in which the worry is couched. The race of men that will follow us may be able to use their language more realistically and specifically, and their lives should therefore be much more free from fear than ours. Their education will train them to handle language symbols and, thus, will enable them automatically to govern their emotions with precision. Deep psychotherapy, for those who can afford it, enables the person to achieve the same ability even now. With determination and effort, and the support of the psychiatrist, the emotionally sick person gradually learns to test the reality of the emotional statements he makes to himself. Those of us who are not sick need not wait for the age of superman, nor need we put ourselves on the couch. Surely, we can learn in some degree to examine those sentences in which we code our fear and guilt and hostility.

Emotionally poisoned speech often floods through our being in waves. We seldom say "Oh, how I hate him" just once to ourselves; we say it again and again and again. We almost hypnotize ourselves with the refrain. Like Tam O'Shanter's wife, we "nurse our wrath to keep it warm." The circling statements intensify as they spiral. Irritation turns into anger and anger into fury as the hypnotic self-suggestion dulls our critical powers. Finally we explode into aggressive or self-destructive behaviors which later we may regret or find unexplainable. Whenever we notice ourselves saying things over and over again to ourselves, we should hear the warning siren. Brooding over wrongs never makes them right.

At one time our students collected a thousand samples of the emotionally toned utterances they had overheard in their dormitories. Over 70 per cent of them were expressions of anger—a sad commentary on the frustrations of college life. A little over 10 per cent were expressions of anxiety; only 1 per cent reflected guilt, and the rest (19 per cent) concerned joyous experiences. We do not at all believe that the proportion actually reflected the true relationship. We are certain that anxieties and guilt amount to more than 11 per cent of our daily quota of feelings. It is just that in our culture these emotions are not verbalized as freely. Indeed, they are most often denied verbalization even in self-communication. They are the unmentionable, the unspeakable. Tragically, such repression does not contribute any peace. Emotions that are buried wordlessly only fester; sooner or later, they break out in behavior.

Another of the findings of this study was revealing. The great majority of the expressions of anger were more ejaculations than verbalizations. They were not so much speech as cries and growls. Most of them were profane. Few of them consisted of more than a single word or phrase. Even the curses were colorless, trite, and without real meaning or pertinence. Surely, our language is not so barren of vocabulary that our angers must be coded nondescriptly. If we must spit bile let us do it eloquently. We remember Shakespeare's "The devil damn thee black, thou cream-faced loon; where gottest thou that goose look?" and one of the passages from Rabelais which contained three hundred and six consecutive words of precise derogation. But most of us are almost helpless when we need to express our anger and frustration. Because we cannot find the words, we get little relief. We can only curse, dully. As a consequence, our emotions find little outlet save in actions that hurt others or hurt ourselves. The more intense the emotion, the better should be the verbalization thereof—if we are ever to learn to live like civilized beings and if we are ever to create a world which is safe. We can only hope that we are the primitive ancestors of a race that will be thoroughly educated to symbolize emotions with ease and precision. The crucial point is that symbols can be scrutinized, manipulated, and rearranged. In contrast, we have little control over the squirting of our glands. If those squirtings can be symbolized appropriately we can handle them. The mouth is our best safety valve, but most of us have not yet learned to use its enormous potential.

The Role of Drama

That man has recognized this vital function of speech for several thousand years is evidenced by his invention of and devotion to drama. Even though he himself finds it very difficult to put his emotions into words, he finds in the theater not only the whole gamut of his feelings but also their expression in language. Through close identification with the actors and through the medium of speech, modern men, like the ancient Greeks, are enabled to experience vicariously the griefs and terrors and joys that are their own. What deep urges within us demand this universal need for drama? We would answer that man has always searched for the verbalization of his emotions. Dimly, he has always yearned for the magical tool with which to control himself. Somehow he has always possessed the knowledge that his salvation lies somewhere in the spoken word. And so, throughout the centuries, he has treasured the works of Aeschylus and Euripides and Sophocles and Shakespeare and Molière and the host of other giants who somehow were able to transform our rages and griefs and exaltations into words.

Why did those ancient Greeks sit on the hard stone seats to witness lust and anger and hate and guilt? Why did the Elizabethans spend so much time on the boards of the Globe Theatre fascinated by the panorama of human emotion unrolled before them by Shakespeare's players? What glues us now to the cushioned seats of the modern theater? The Greeks called it catharsis: the cleansing of the self by identification with the players as they portray the storms of emotion which all of us know to some degree.

But such abreaction, the vicarious acting out of emotions, is also a teaching device. Empathized emotions are not enough. We need to say the words. We need the special genius of the dramatist to reflect in the utterances of his actors the true state of our own feelings. This is what we yearn for; this is what each of us needs so badly—some way to put into words the emotions that buffet us. We feel so mute, so helpless. We can only ache and suffer, we can only mutter or cry. But we may yet learn how to verbalize our feelings as the Greeks did from hearing Antigone's despairing words "Unwept, unwedded, unbefriended, alone, pitilessly abused, I am dragged to my death." And those of us who can say little more than "What's the use?" may learn how to express the ultimate in pessimism: "Tomorrow and tomorrow and tomorrow,/Creeps in this petty pace from day to day,/To the last syllable of recorded time;/ And all our yesterdays have lighted fools/The way to dusty death. Out, out, brief candle!/Life's but a walking shadow, a poor player/ That struts and frets his hour upon the stage/And then is heard no more: it is a tale/Told by an idiot, full of sound and fury,/Signifying nothing." These overly familiar words of Shakespeare, read or memorized by every schoolboy, still hold tremendous power because of our deep hunger for ways to express the futility which every man must experience at some time in his life. We need to learn the words that release our stormy depths. Perhaps in some far future day, even the ordinary man will be able to use his language to know the deep recesses of his being, and knowing, be their master. Surely even now we may find, by steeping ourselves in our literature and drama, some small hint of what is to come. Surely even now we can begin.

Speech and Psychotherapy

When we confront people bedeviled by deep emotional conflicts, once again we are awed by the tremendous potential that speech possesses. It is the basic tool of all psychotherapy. "Words are the physicians of a diseased mind," wrote Aeschylus. The clinical psychologist and the psychiatrist alike rely upon talking as their primary healing agent, and it is the patient who does most of the talking. Some scrutiny of the therapeutic process may help us appreciate this function which we take so much for granted. And perhaps we may learn how to use our own speech to solve many of our own emotional problems.

The people who go to a psychotherapist for help are usually in deep trouble. They are miserable, consumed with anxiety or guilt or suspicion or some other variety of unpleasant emotion. Often they are unable to maintain normal social relationships; they are maladjusted and unhappy and so are their associates. The complaints that they present are so many and so varied that to recite them here would fill many pages. An old Finnish proverb says that Evil has a thousand faces; certainly the evil that is emotional illness has many more.

Usually the possessors of these emotional problems are unable to recognize what the problems really are. The presented symptoms are often only masks behind which the true difficulties lie. Those bedeviled by unverbalized emotion say they can't sleep or can't study or have devastating fears or are depressed or find it difficult to breathe or think terrible thoughts or possess any number of other miseries. Often they are incoherent, unable to define their problem in any way save that of helpless desperation.

Problems must be defined to be solved, and it is the task of the psychotherapist to help his patient do that defining through speech. The psychiatrist accomplishes this through very skillful questioning, the clinical psychologist by reflecting back to the patient the feelings being expressed, and the psychoanalyst primarily through the sufferer's free association and dreams. The methods vary but the vehicle is the same; it is through the analytical verbalization of his past and present feelings and the circumstances that precipitate them that the patient finally returns to mental health. Speech is the medication.

Perhaps a few glimpses of the therapeutic process would be

useful here. In the following example, a stutterer is having a counseling interview with the psychologist. We pick it up midstream:

> ABE: Well, my old man wasn't sure he was getting his money's worth so he had to come along for the first couple sessions with the speech therapist. Made me feel like I was in short pants, a kid, a grade school kid, damn him. . . .
>
> COUNSELOR: Burned you up, eh. . . ?
>
> ABE: Yeah. Never would treat me like I had any brains or was grown up. . . . He was always the big stuff. . . . Don't think I ever told you before but he's a stutterer too.
>
> COUNSELOR: That right?
>
> ABE: He isn't too bad though. Claims he cured himself, by will power . . . says if I had guts God gave a rooster I'd cure myself too. . . . I've caught him hiding it plenty of times though. . . .
>
> COUNSELOR: He hasn't any right to put on such an act. . . .
>
> ABE: Nah, but he does . . . and he gets away with it too. But I can see through him and his little tricks, using an easy word instead of a hard one . . . and coughing to cover up when he's stuck. Doesn't fool me a bit. . . .
>
> COUNSELOR: You're onto him. . . .
>
> ABE: Yeah, but what really corks me is that he acts as though I'm a dummy because I still keep stuttering sometimes. I got a good job as an accountant. . . . Make more money than he does even. . . . But he talks better. . . . I talk awful sometimes. Maybe I don't have the guts or brains or something. . . . Why can't I just tell myself: "Stop that stuttering. Be a man for once. . . ." *

In this small fragment of a counseling session, we see the person just beginning to define his problem, just touching on a few of its features. In earlier interviews he had spoken copiously of his happy home, his wonderful father, and his fears of speaking. Here he is putting into words some of the feelings he had previously found it difficult to confront, his self-concept as a weak, immature, inadequate child; the hostility toward his father and the need to blame him; the speech impotence as a sign of unmanliness. Note the unusual phrase "What really corks me," and its possible relationship to stuttering. Here we see the healing power of speech at work. Unstated emotional problems cannot be solved; occasionally, through environmental changes, they may be resolved. But speech is the prime psychotherapeutic tool. Only by putting a problem into symbolic verbal

* Charles Van Riper and Leslie Gruber, *A Casebook in Stuttering* (New York: Harper and Row, Publishers, 1953), p. 23.

form can it be objectified so that the necessary manipulations can be accomplished to produce a solution.

Some of our emotional conflicts are so profound or so deeply repressed that they cannot be identified through interviews such as we have illustrated. The feelings are so unspeakable, so untouchable, that the psychotherapist must have recourse to a methodology which suspends the value judgments most of us pass upon our verbal output. Sigmund Freud, that towering genius who probably had more effect upon our culture in this century than any other man, discovered that by asking his patients to freely associate—to say whatever they were thinking about at the moment without censorship of any kind—emotional content could be made available which was not accessible by any other means. The ability to do this free association is not easily acquired. It requires the patient to stop all monitoring, to let his thoughts roam where they will, to phrase whatever "comes into his head," no matter how bizarre or meaningless it may appear. Often we find verbal imagery and metaphor of extreme vividness. Here is a sample of what one person said as he verbalized the thoughts that flitted through his mind. The material has been structured somewhat to make it more readable:

> There are two people on horses and they have a rope tied around their necks connecting themselves. They want to go in different directions and kick their horses. The two people look exactly alike. They kick their horses and are pulled off and they try to run in opposite directions, only they can't get apart and can't agree on where to go. I think one is trying to go toward a swamp where there are all kinds of birds, crocodiles and stuff. The one that doesn't want to go to the swamp has a black mask over his face. But he still looks like the other one. These Siamese twins here. One wants to bathe and the other hates to bathe. He won't let the other one take a bath. There is a book and one of the pages wishes it were a different page. If it were a different page it would mix up the book, but it still wants to be a different page. There's this colt that was just born. Its belly button is still attached to its mother and he wants it separated, but mother doesn't because she wants her colt around her. There are two people and they are handcuffed together and they hate each other. They kill each other because they can't get away from each other. There's this spring and it's being kept together, only it wants to get open and can't. Now there's a person driving a black Ford up the mountains where there are curves. He didn't like to go around the turns so he goes straight over the mountains and smashed into a tree. He had been in prison before and had promised to go straight. He went

straight—that's how he interpreted it. There are two people standing on a fence, and each wants the other one to get off but neither will, so one starts shaking the real thin fence and then the other one starts to shake the fence and they both fall off. . . .*

All of us have known moments of ambivalence in the roles we must play. The person who said the above was expressing the tug-of-war that had been tearing him apart and making it impossible for him to function normally in society. He was not insane. Using his free association of ideas he was merely putting into colorful words the stress that he was feeling. He was saying whatever passed through his mind. By doing so, he was bringing up from the depths of his being the repressed emotions that had driven him into behaviors which prevented him from adjusting appropriately to life's demands. Eventually, he was able to interpret and to understand what he was saying about himself, and to make the necessary changes. All this just by talking!

Free association can be tremendously exhausting because as the words pour out the person experiences the feelings that they express. Many of these feelings have been buried so deep within the tissues of the mind that one can almost hear the tearing of those tissues. It is not a pleasant experience to have to relive old agonies, even if they are disguised in metaphor. But once resubmitted to the light of reality, they lose their power. And then comes relief, blessed peace for the moment, and the opportunity to create a new life free from the tyranny of the glands. All the pharmacopeia we possess holds no healing potion so potent as speech.

Let us give one more illustration of how, through speech, the crucial insights necessary for resolving our emotional conflicts can emerge. A friend of ours, a psychoanalyst, told us about a recurring dream which one of his patients had repeatedly experienced, the understanding of which changed her whole life for the better. The patient was quite sane but had numerous depressions and anxieties. A very attractive girl, she had also been married three times before the age of twenty-three, each time to a man much older than herself. This was the dream:

I dreamed I was at home and my mother was out. And my father came in smiling and said, "I've got some medicine for you." I told him I wasn't sick but he said yes I was and I had to take

---

* From *Handbook of Speech Pathology* (pp. 942–43), edited by Lee Edward Travis. Copyright © 1957 by Appleton-Century-Crofts, Inc. Reprinted by permission of Appleton-Century-Crofts.

> it. And he had it in his hand. And he started to come toward me holding it out. Then I knew in a flash it was poison and he was going to kill me. And I tried to run but I couldn't. My legs wouldn't move. And he put it up to my mouth but I shook my head and he couldn't. And then he somehow got on my back and was reaching around to put it, the poison, in my mouth. And I told him no, that I'd kill him, that he'd better get off my back. But he wouldn't and he kept trying to put the poison in my mouth, and so suddenly I bent down and flung him over my head hard so he crashed to the floor. And he lay there still. And I saw he was dead, that I'd killed him. But in his outstretched hand there on the floor I saw, not poison, but two jelly beans. It was candy, not poison, he was trying to give me. He was trying to tell me he loved me.

We have cited these illustrations from psychopathology to make a point that has pertinence for all of us. Most of us have no need for the psychotherapist, but we do have a need for speech as a healing tool. We can use it every day as a safety valve for our emotional pressures, as a method for defining the minor emotional conflicts that make our lives less happy than they might otherwise be, and finally for formulating plans so that in the future we will be less vulnerable. Must we deny ourselves this function of speech until we are terribly sick? Perhaps, if we can learn to use this potent tool wisely, we may become models for our children, and they in turn for their own, so that one day, far in the future, man can live in harmony with himself.

Storing Happiness

But speech is more than mere incantation to exorcize our evil emotions and give us a precarious peace. With a net of words we can also capture exaltation. Our poets and dramatists again have shown us the way. But how poorly do our ordinary tongues catch and hold our better moments! "How about that!" we exclaim. "Isn't that pretty?" "I love you, Lulu Belle!" Life is full of moments that should be stored and treasured, but we must remember that our memories are primarily verbal ones. Images fade, most sounds cannot be echoed for long once they are gone, the feel of a loving hand soon vanishes. François Villon, the thief-poet of France, cried out in metaphor his protest five hundred years ago: "Ou sont les neiges d'antan?" (Where are the snows of yesteryear?) It is words that comprise the magic of memory whereby the good moments can be held and savored anew.

We knew a little old lady once whose face was beautiful and serene despite some eighty years that had held much tragedy. We asked her secret. "I'm not sure it's any secret," she replied. "But every night after I'm in bed and before I go to sleep, I tell myself about every single good thing that happened to me during the day. It might only be the look on a child's face or the smell of new bread or the wind melody in the eaves, but I remember and I live it again that way." We feel that the key to her serenity and zest for life lay in this verbalization. She had learned to fix the flux of transient experience by coding it in words. She told us that during the day, when good things happened, she turned them into words so that she could remember them that night. "Sometimes I'm a bit embarrassed," she told us, "because occasionally I talk aloud to myself about these things and then other people think I'm getting senile. So I try not to do it aloud when other people are around. But I do it to myself anyway. It's harder than you think, too, hard to get just the right words so that it will stick, but I'm getting better at it. Had a hard time this morning describing to myself how our pine tree outside the window looked with the white wool afghan of new snow keeping it warm."

We have known few people so young at heart or who lived so well so long. Perhaps she had learned what the human race must learn—that the only way to hold the good of existence is through the alchemy of words.

This, of course, is the poet's way. Alas, we make the way of the poet very difficult in our culture, though we treasure in our literature a hundred thousand of the crucial moments in their lives—the good moments that they had the genius to seize and fix forever in words. Most children have the gift also, speaking of flames as "fire curls," of windowpanes as "hard holes," of "shaving the ground" with a mower, until the asbestos curtain of our culture comes down and we insist that they stop talking to themselves or stop talking nonsense. Must we be forever the race that Vachel Lindsay described in these words:

Let not young souls be smothered out before
They do quaint deeds and fully flaunt their pride,
It is the world's one crime its babes grow dull,
Its poor are ox-like, limp and leaden-eyed.*

* Reprinted with permission of The Macmillan Company from *The Congo and Other Poems* (p. 65) by Vachel Lindsay. Copyright 1914 by The Macmillan Company. Copyright renewed 1942 by Elizabeth C. Lindsay.

All of us are poor who are leaden-eyed or grey-tongued with triteness. Yet there is hope! Witness the section on picturesque speech in the *Reader's Digest*. Most of us, if we realize the value thereof, can verbalize our joys as well as our sorrows. We need not code the experiences in rhyme or meter but surely, if we try, we can preserve them by verbalizing, if not to others, then to ourselves.

It is difficult for many of us to share our better emotions in any words at all. How many middle-aged wives grow dumpy because their husbands never tell them that they are beautiful? How many husbands come home dead tired after the day's battles to find no words of comfort or endearment? Even apple pie is not enough! How many children thirst for praise and reassurance? How many lovers are mute?

This is not as it should be. Even a dog will respond to a kind word. Inhibition of appreciation and affection is no better for mental health than is inhibition of aciduous emotions. The stern code of our Nordic Calvinistic forbears needs revision. We need more Latin in our loving and in our living. We need to be more spontaneous and free in our verbalization of devotion and esteem. Most of the bonds we forge that unite us are made stronger through the words we speak to each other in affection. Surely, it is not too late to learn to talk.

In olden times, most of the nobility had their gossips—individuals whom they could trust to share their confidences. Many of us are fortunate enough to have close acquaintances who can provide the same sort of ears. And, among the better things that come from a successful marriage is the communion of sharing through speech not only the larger joys, but the smaller ones. We need not communicate these only to ourselves if we can find companions who will also appreciate them. Troubles shared are divided but shared joys are multiplied. Little children seem to know this instinctively. So, too, do the old men, telling the tales of their youth over and over again to anyone who will listen.

Perhaps that future race that will inhabit the earth and far-off space will be trained to express their emotions more easily than we can. Perhaps these men of tomorrow will not need to tangle themselves in our emotional traps because they will have learned to symbolize them in terms that permit solutions. It is conceivable that they may have a new vocabulary for their emotional states, rich enough so that they will not need to speak in metaphor and parable.

After all, the Eskimo has been able to invent many words for different kinds of snow, although he has no word for snow itself. But even now we can begin. If we can only realize the immense potential for emotional fulfillment and control that is possessed by the spoken word, we can lead better lives and create better models for our young. And we can hope then that man can bring under control that last frontier—himself.

3 The Search for Identity: Egocentric Speech

When, with an ear slightly askew so that it can truly listen, we scrutinize the torrent of talk that ebbs and flows about us, we note with some surprise that a very large portion of that speech is being employed for purposes other than the communication of information. All these people seem to be talking about themselves—sometimes almost *to* themselves. With this insight comes a second one: Much of our own speech is similarly egocentric. It is the thesis of this chapter that egocentric speech fulfills the deep human need to know who we are. If we can understand this immensely important power possessed by speech, we may be able to exercise it more effectively for our own fulfillment.

The perpendicular pronoun *I* is perhaps the most dominant, if not the most frequent, word in the speech of that mouthy mammal, man. Researchers Henle and Hubbel(1) recorded many samples of adult conversation, and they found that the egocentric pronouns, *I, me, my, mine,* and *myself,* occurred in from 30 to 40 per cent of all the remarks spoken by their subjects. Another researcher (who shall be nameless here) procured the data for his unpublished master's thesis by boring a hole in the floor of his apartment, inserting a microphone, and recording everything that was said in the apartment below. In this lower apartment lived a "typical American family," consisting of a father, mother, and two children—a son and a daughter. The researcher recorded everything that they said for a month and then spent a year analyzing his data. He concluded finally that most of what had been said (81.3 per cent) in that family during that time consisted of sentences about the self. Anyone with an analytical ear would not be surprised at his findings. As the poet Walt Whitman wrote, sounding his barbaric yawp over the roofs of the world, "I celebrate myself and sing myself."

Listen, if you will, to the staccato of the perpendicular pronoun in the speech about you: "And I said to him, I said. . . ." "I'm the kind of person who. . . ." "I think that. . . ." The *I*'s explode like popcorn in the conversational pan. Indeed, it is difficult to speak without them. To test this statement, we assigned some of our students the project of determining how long they could resist the use of one or another of the egocentric pronouns during an entire morning. Not a single one was able to prevent the occurrence of these pronouns for more than half an hour of conversation, and most of them slipped within five minutes. One girl plaintively protested that we'd almost made her mute, and another reported hesitant speech to a degree that resembled stuttering.

Egocentric speech pervades all ordinary communication; it is found in every mouth. Self-reference is the keynote to our verbal melody; we wander away from it on occasion, but over and over again we return to it. You will hear egocentricity in the casual conversation of the man on the street, in the shrill chatter of a cocktail party, and more softly in the murmuring of two lovers in the moonlight. Into the black cups of a million telephones go ten million *I*'s each day. In every store and business and school in the land we hear speech centered about the self. Surely something so universal must serve some basic purpose.

The Heart of the Matter

More than two thousand years ago, Socrates uttered a prescription for the ills of mankind that we still find fundamental, though difficult to fulfill. It was "Know thyself!" In every generation, the baby in the crib, exploring his fingers and toes, seeking to define the image of his body so that he can control it, is responding to that universal command. Since the dawn of history, man's progress has been measured by his mastery of the unknown. Yet the major mystery remains—man's own nature. Each of us in his own way must do what he can to understand who he is. Unfortunately, most of us are at least partial strangers to ourselves. We know what we look like because we have viewed ourselves in mirrors and photographs, but in large measure the person within the skin escapes us. Often we define ourselves only through the words with which other people have described us and those, as we have said earlier, may be distorted words. We must not know ourselves only through our reflection in *their* flawed mirrors. When our self-concepts are false, then troubles come. Across the barrier of two thousand years Socrates still speaks to each of us.

Speech and Self-knowledge

But how may we ever come to know ourselves? Once again, the way is the speech way. We explore ourselves by word of mouth. We carry on a constant dialogue with ourselves. We comment on what we perceive or do or feel. Through this commentary, silent and otherwise, we revise our self-images as we are changed by the experiences we undergo. Each of us possesses a private picture of himself, sometimes several pictures. We have an ideal self-image which we often try to convince others is the real person that bears our name. And we have another self-image that we know comes closer to the reality. This is much harder for us to confront or to exhibit. These pictures are constantly being repainted, not only by ourselves but by others. Every time we meet a new person we create, through our words, a self-picture. Then we hand him the brush and try to comprehend the picture of us that he sketches. We draw many verbal pictures of ourselves in the course of a lifetime; we play many parts, trying on one role after another until we discover those that fit us best, until finally we create a self-concept that we and others can accept.

We who take our talk so casually have only a dim awareness of the immense utility of speech in the development and maintenance of our sense of self. Tiny specks in a vast ocean of space, we manage to feel important. In the eternity of time, it would appear impossible that the tiny durations of our lives could hold meaning. How can we achieve any sense of meaningful identity in the context of such infinities as these? Yet we do—and we do so through speech. Through the use of symbols, we are able to divide that tiny tick of time into minutes and hours that, at least when we are young, seem quite sufficient for our needs. And through the use of language, we also come to have a sense of self which makes us, to ourselves at least, the most valuable specks of matter in the universe.

This enormous human achievement of giving ourselves significant identity appears even more incredible when we consider that each of us is constantly changing. Like a flame, we are never the same from one moment to another. The cells of our bodies are in constant flux, as are the cells of the people about us. How then do we maintain the integrity of our identities so that we can feel important? Again the answer will be found in our words.

Speech and the Body Image

Central to self-concept is the *body image*. Each of us feels that the essence of our individuality is somehow encompassed by the skin. "This is me," or "Here I am!" we say and point to our midriffs, as centering the whole. But the infant does not arrive in this world with this perception of his body as the core of his being. He learns separateness at his mother's knee or in her arms. She touches his eyes and ears and nose, which he cannot see, and she names them. She teaches him in turn to point to these and to his fingers and toes when she calls them out. As she bathes or fondles him, she talks about washing his arms and his legs and his little bottom. As she feeds him she tells him to put the spoon in his mouth, not in his ear. "Put your foot in the snowsuit, now!" she commands, and soon he will be telling himself to do it. If you will listen to the self-talk of a two- or three-year-old, you will hear him commanding his body to do things he wishes it to do: "Johnny, get up! Johnny fall down! Johnny put finger in water."

These remarks may appear to possess little importance, but what the parent and child are doing, quite unconsciously, is building the child's basic schema of his *self*. The body image is not at first a visual one; it is a verbal construct, built out of names and commands. Only later will the child come to recognize himself in photographs or mirrors, and even then the experience means little unless it is accompanied by the appropriate verbal labels. Anthropologists tell us that the adults of primitive tribes do not recognize their own photographs, a finding that should not surprise those of us who have had to make a choice from several photographs of our own faces. The body image is essentially a verbal one.

We must not fail to recognize the significance of this fact. There are too many lost souls roaming the earth, unintegrated individuals who do not know who they really are, people with split personalities, persons who reject themselves. If, because the mother must work in a factory or because she must place her child in a rejecting home or an uncaring institution, the child fails to get the necessary loving commentary on the contours and movements of his body parts, that child may remain forever a human Humpty-Dumpty that not even the king's men could put together. None of us is perfectly integrated at best, but it should be every child's birthright to have a coherent body image as the basis of his personality.

Throughout our lives our body images, and the way we and other people talk about them, determine much of our security or insecurity. Consider how vulnerable we are to comments about such things as the possession of a large nose, obesity, scars, or acne, to say nothing of such major distortions of the body image produced by arthritis or the loss of an eye or a limb. Yet all hunchbacks are not from Notre Dame. Those who can triumph over physical deviations manage to do so through the magic of speech, knowing with Burns that "a man's a man for all that." Throughout our lives our bodies are subjected to insults as well as to physiological changes, and unless we are able to reconcile these changes and to fit them into our identity with a minimum of pain, we live lives less rich and resourceful than they might be. We may thank our gods that we have in speech the mechanism for such philosophy.

We should also recognize that we are equally vulnerable to verbal praise so far as the body image is concerned. We have known women who built thwarted lives on a foundation of "naturally curly hair" that had been overpraised in childhood. We have known men who, because they learned early that they were males and that this difference was the only one of importance, misspent their lives proving the obvious, and missed much else. Psychoanalysts point out how many maladjustments stem from overreward, from fixations at levels less than those of maturity. They call our attention to the hypochondriacs and food addicts and narcissists who are so overconcerned with their bodies because of their fixations. The verbal approval of others is a powerful force which we must understand—and sometimes resist lest it shape our growth abnormally or fixate us at levels far below our potential. Many of us still dance compulsively to the pipers of our past without regard to the current pertinence of the tunes. If we are to have fulfillment, we must break free from some of the verbal shackles of our childhood.

Speech and Learning New Roles

We have spoken of the body image as the core of the personality. About this core cluster many roles, each defined and made manifest through language. As we play each part, we say different things and speak differently. Watch the three- or four-year-old at play! At one moment he is a baby, at another with his father's hat, he is his own parent; at still another, he is a doctor, a teacher, a policeman, or even the family cat. All these roles are characteristically accompanied by postures, noises, and self-talk characteristic of the model with which he is identifying.

This play acting in children is not to be discouraged. It is their way of exploring potential for growth and change. The little girl baking her sand pies and the little boy shaving with his toothbrush are sampling their future roles. It is fascinating to hear them in such play, using the words and gestures and intonations of their parents. This is not mere monkey-like imitation; it is identification. At the moment the boy *is* his father, with all the power and privileges pertaining thereto. A moment or two later, of course, he will be a child again and this, too, is an important discovery. He learns thereby that he has a choice of roles, that he can play many parts yet still remain himself, that he can change his behavior without losing his identity. All this through speech!

Perhaps because they were deprived of such identifications in early childhood, far too many children become rigid adults, unable to make the changes and adjustments that life demands. They cling to old roles, often infantile ones, that once were useful, and they fear to attempt the new ones demanded of them by circumstances. As we change and as our life situation changes, we cannot possibly fulfill our potential by clinging to the old garments our personalities have outgrown. Each new role is an unfolding of a new aspect of self. If we are to know ourselves as Socrates commanded, we must know not only the bodily core but the entire bundle of roles about that core, some already revealed and some held in potential for future growth.

Because it is so important that we accept the utter necessity of change, we feel we should perhaps speak further concerning the reasons for the resistance which all of us feel when we find ourselves compelled to assume a new role. Basically this resistance reflects a universal principle: All systems attempt to maintain their integrity, they react so as to minimize a disturbance, they try to maintain the status quo.

Our self-concepts are no exceptions. Self-preservation refers to more than physical survival; the human being also seeks to maintain the integrity of his *self*. This is why the crucial changes in physical development—when the baby becomes the child, the child the adolescent, the youth the man, the time of menopause or loss of virility—all cause upheavals. The core of our personalities, our body images, then change. But we must also recognize that some of the same discomfort occurs whenever we are forced to undertake new roles. Although change is the law of life, it always poses some threat to the identity, and so we resist. We experience always the need to preserve our *selves* as well as our bodies, and the easiest way to do this is to stay within the old roles.

Ouspensky, the Russian author, says it better than we can:

> The study of the roles a man plays represents a very necessary part of self knowledge. Each man's repertoire is very limited. And if a man simply says "I" or "Ivan Ivanich" he will not see the whole of himself because "Ivan Ivanich" also is not one; a man has at least five or six roles. One or two for his family, one or two at his office (one for his subordinates and another for his superiors), one for friends in a restaurant, and perhaps one who is interested in exalted ideas and likes intellectual conversation. And at different times the man is fully identified with one role and is unable to separate himself from it. To see the roles, to know one's repertoire, particularly to know its limitations, is to know a great deal. But the point is that, outside his repertoire, a man feels very uncomfortable should something push him if only temporarily out of his rut, and he tries his hardest to return to one of his usual roles.*

Yet there is more to life than either ruts or survival. To fulfill ourselves we must grow; we must change. The people about us change; we leave our parents behind; we discover new persons who play other important parts in our existence; our environments shift. New roles are demanded of us, and if we refuse them we lose more than we maintain. The satisfactory self is like a human embryo, con-

---

* P. D. Ouspensky, *In Search of the Miraculous* (New York: Harcourt, Brace & World, Inc., 1948) (pp. 239–40). By permission of the publishers.

stantly changing its contours, developing new structures and functions, always growing yet always remaining intact. Our defensive protest against having to explore and accept new roles can be understood well enough by all of us. We may fear that we will not play them well enough, that our awkwardness and inadequacy will be revealed. But this is always true of all new patterns of behavior. So we must explore and experiment, learning how to talk as well as act like a man, to find the words for the role of lover, to acquire the voice of authority, responsibility, and command. Each new role demands new forms of expression, and though at first we falter, at last we speak surely. The new father holds his first-born with gingerly clumsiness, yet eventually he even learns to change a diaper. At first he does not know how to talk as a father should, but soon he manages that part as previously he learned to speak as a husband—which is to say, very little. The student becomes a teacher and his manner of speaking changes. The peremptory dictation of a businessman is not heard in the garden of his home. Somehow we learn to speak our many parts with eventual ease, to vary them appropriately with our differing listeners. The well-adjusted person is he who can reveal that part of his multifaceted nature which is in tune with the demands of a new situation.

We need to talk to many different people in many different circumstances if we are to fulfill our self-potentials. Each new situation requires that we respond a bit differently, that we modify our patterns of speech behavior appropriately. So we change; so we grow. Each man is a river, gathering new flood and fertility from all the lands it passes through till last it reaches sea. We become a part of all the men we meet, and they of us if we but join ourselves to them through speech. Only through speech can we have the communion that permits our potential selves to unfold. We are told to read, to travel, and to go to college in order to "broaden" ourselves. If there is growth from such experiences, it is probably a broadening of the self-concept due to the accumulation of new roles.

How Speech Leads to Self-knowledge

When psychologists are faced with the task of getting to know a certain person, they employ a variety of tests and conduct interviews concerning the past history of that client. Most of these tests demand verbal responses. The MMPI (Minnesota Multiphasic Personality Inventory), for example, consists of a huge battery of items, each one containing an egocentric statement such as: "I have never done anything dangerous for the thrill of it," or "I believe I am being followed." If you were the client, perhaps you might be given the Rorschach test, a series of ink-blots which you are to look at and tell what you imagine each ink-blot represents. Then the psychologist will ask you to talk. It will be what you say that will enable him to know you. Or he may give you the T-A-T, a series of picture cards, and ask you to make up a story about each. Again he wants your speech. Or perhaps he might administer the W-A-Y, merely asking you a very simple question, "Who-Are-You?," and insisting that you answer it with the responses that come spontaneously into your mind, one after another. The spouse of one of your authors, a strong woman (to say it softly), answered that question by serially saying, "Your wife . . . a woman . . . your wife . . . a mother . . . your . . . ," and was angry for a week as she recognized the hierarchy of dominance in the roles. Furthermore, she was not mollified to learn that her husband had never used the word "husband" in any of his responses. But our point is that it is impossible to know who another person is, or who we are, except through the medium of language. We reveal ourselves to others and to ourselves through speech.

Confrontation and Revelation

Whenever we meet a new acquaintance or join an already functioning group we must expose ourselves. Perhaps any new confrontation always holds some uncertainty or some measure of anxiety in our society. Do we shake hands to demonstrate, as some have claimed, that the right hand holds no knife? When we speak to a new listener or group, we know we are being scanned and evaluated. Will the stranger or the group or the audience accept us, and in what fashion? This is always the moment for revelation, for displaying the role, that particular side of self, which is most likely to be acceptable.

Doubtless this is why most students find it hard to enroll in a speech class, and harder yet to get up that first time and speak. The world seems full of eyeballs, all focused upon the speaker, examining and evaluating, accepting or rejecting. Usually of course, this is an exaggerated perception. Most of those eyeballs are glazed with disinterest or turned inward with self-concern. But we know, we always know at that moment of confrontation, that when we talk we will reveal ourselves.

By the time we become adults, most of us are more or less reconciled to this scanning in ordinary communication. When we get up to speak formally however, tension begins to sizzle within us. The naïve beginner is under the illusion that he alone suffers so, but even the most practiced speaker has the same experience, if not in the same form or degree. He who speaks must inevitably invite the scanning of the listener. Perhaps, if in the history of mankind no single soul had ever told a lie or posed a threat, this scrutiny of the person would never have become so prevalent. But we who speak must accept assessment by our listeners as a matter of course, and not be traumatized by it. Indeed, the greatest potential value in public speaking is this training in the sharpening of one's awareness of his identity. The good speaker meets the challenge and hears a silent trumpet that brings out his best. There are some, of course, who pretend that no horn has sounded, who almost deny that they have listeners, who speak only to those enchanted listeners—themselves. These people rarely speak well, and they do not communicate, even though thereby they hide their essential fear. There are others who try to flee the challenge, avoiding any sort of speaking situation where their impoverished egos may be displayed. But life lies in wait for these escapists. Only the hermit in the Ozarks or the Trappist monk with his eternal vow of silence can hope to avoid successfully all demands for speech before some scanning listener. If we run away we do so at our peril, for avoidance begets fear and fear in turn more avoidance and fear, and then when circumstances inevitably force us to confront the eyeballs, our performance will be really abject. So most of us accept our fate as speakers and, like the bird accepts his wings when it leaves the nest, we do the best we can to learn how to speak before our fellows with some ease and facility. We would doubtlessly prefer to master the skills alone and privately, but most of us recognize that this is impossible. We must exhibit our selves whether we wish to or not. We say "Ecce homo" (Behold the man!) whenever we open our mouths to speak.

The Introductory Function of Egocentric Speech

Yet egocentric speech need not be egotistical and it usually is not. Essentially, its major function in a speaking situation is introductory. Observe how swiftly the personal pronouns fly back and forth when two strangers begin to talk to each other. Even in formal speaking, after you have been introduced by some person who often seems possessed by some devilish need to put you in a false position, you will feel compelled to talk a bit about yourself to put things straight. Since your speech will reveal you anyway, it is wise to use it immediately for that purpose. You have nothing to lose except your pretenses. You know more about the topic of yourself than anyone else; the words and ideas will flow easily if you are not playing games with your audience. Wallow if you must in perpendicular pronouns, but use the opportunity presented by the confrontation to explore the person behind the façade of your skin. People are interested in people, and they will be interested in you.

We do not wish to end this discussion with the implication that the sole usefulness of egocentric speech lies in its ability to make you feel more comfortable in speaking before a speech class. There are more confrontations than this in life where it will prove a valuable tool—if you learn to use it well. In finding a job or a companion or a mate we must first introduce ourselves. It seems to us that in all our present educational system there exists no better opportunity for learning to understand one another than exists in the various offerings of a college department of speech. The first course in speech enables us to introduce ourselves intimately to a group of our fellow human beings and to understand the dynamics of that confrontation. Here we have the freedom to expose and explore ourselves in relative safety since all others are equally challenged in the same way. Here we can use our egocentric speech to identify and discover our various facets of self. In interpretive reading and dramatics, creative or theatrical, we can experiment with new roles to determine our potentials and to encourage flexibility. In debate and discussion we find opportunities for being able to take the role of the other, so necessary for appropriate variance. In public address, we learn how to identify with larger groups. In all of these, we find the human mirrors we need to know ourselves.

Speech and Self-escape

Some speakers use their speech not to discover but to cover. They cannot bear to let others really know who they are, probably because they cannot bear the self-confrontation that comes by reflection. Some of these resemble magicians, deft and quick with their verbal sleight of hand, using their speech to conceal rather than to reveal themselves. Some of these speech magicians are tremendously glib. They seem to be able to speak fluently and copiously on any subject, in any situation, and for any length of time. When they have finished their almost compulsive logorrhea, however, it is very difficult to know what they have said. It is also difficult to know very much about them—which is why they speak that way. They are octopi, squirting a murky torrent of words to conceal themselves. They are not to be envied. An octopus is not usually a treasured companion.

There are also the verbal artists and offstage actors, those who do not dare be themselves and must paint pictures or play false roles instead. Some of these artists who paint pictures of themselves with words become very skillful, and their creations are often attractive. But they are not true. Sooner or later, the fraudulence will be exposed. We have nothing really to offer except ourselves. We are what we are, always with some flaws. Shall we be actors or persons? That is the question. We greatly admire the competence of skilled actors—but only on stage. We have known sad souls who have spent their lives and energies trying to sustain a false illusion about themselves. We have known a few who were able to so immerse themselves in false roles that they sounded completely sincere. But, as Wendell Johnson, the speech pathologist, once remarked, even a cockroach can be sincere. The place for an actor is on the stage, not on the platform or in the discussion group and certainly not in the normal verbal intercourse of living. Let us be ourselves when we speak! Security is the ability to tolerate liabilities and to do the best we can with what we have.

The Exploratory Function of Egocentric Speech

We have said that speech is introductory, that it is used to reveal the speaker. We must also make clear that it has another important function: to probe and test and reveal the listener. Speech, and we will develop this theme later, is a two-way process. There are always messages flowing both ways, even when the listener is silent. His facial expressions, his postures, and his body movements can be eloquent indeed. The speaker who attempts to ignore this feedback is most unwise. Not only will he be likely to lose his listeners in a hurry but, more important still, he loses another chance to know himself. In our search for identity we find it in the mirrors our listeners hold up to us.

The insect has antennae; we have speech. Every new audience, every new listener is an unknown, and the unknown often is colored more or less with threat. Accordingly, when the beginning speaker confronts such a situation he tends to recoil from the threatening audience contact, refusing to look at the listeners, and exposing as little of himself as possible. This is, of course, all wrong, as he will soon learn. What he must do is to use his speech to scan his audience, to explore the unknown, to seek the identification which will enable his message to be understood and accepted.

A skilled and experienced speaker knows this well. Even before he begins, he scrutinizes and listens to the hum of his audience; he learns as much as he can about its composition. Then, when he starts speaking, it is fascinating to watch his verbal radar at work, sending out his speech signals and scanning the feedback, hunting for the little cues that indicate that he and his listeners are in tune. And even after he has achieved this "fix," as the technicians call it, his radar never stops scanning for reduced impact, for rejection, for the first signs of listener loss. When he senses any of these reactions, he varies his output until once again the feedback indicates that he and his audience are one.

This same process can occur even in ordinary conversation. We watch our listeners and examine their verbal responses not only to find out if they understand us, but also to discover whether they accept us. If the aspect of the self we have exhibited in words evokes approval, then we realize that this feature is one that we can cherish. A little anecdote may illustrate this point. One of our students told us this tale:

> All my life I've been shy and mousy. I've been trained for years always to try to please, to hide my resentments, to be nice. Well, the other day I was talking to a boy who was needling me and teasing me, and suddenly, out of the blue, I just up and told him to go to hell. Why, I've never said anything like that in my whole life and I was just sick after I'd said it. But you know what happened? He looked at me with real interest and said, "Boy, I didn't know you had fire in you. Well, well, well." And I've got a date with him tonight!

Similarly, when the things we say create rejection, we learn from these rejecting responses the seamier sides of self, those that we should try to change or inhibit. The more we talk to people, the more we find out who we are. But we must scan our reflections in our listeners' mirrors if we hope to know.

One of the most effective ways of exploring an audience or a listener for these reflections of self is through the use of egocentric speech. People are interested in people. They prick up their ears and respond more visibly when they hear egocentric speech. The personal pronouns and statements about self are little gongs that ring for attention and arouse judgmental responses. The personal anecdote always seems to have some special power in this regard. In egocentric speech we have perhaps the most efficient tool that has been invented for scanning our listeners. By revealing one of our many sides of self and scrutinizing the feedback, we can explore not only our audience but ourselves. If the side of self we show is rejected or ignored, we at least know something very important about our listeners, and we can then show them other facets which they may accept.

Trail's End

Since we continue to change as long as life continues, the search for a fixed identity is probably doomed to failure. Yet at any given period of time we can hope to know the cluster of roles about our body images that we call the self. Such knowledge, with its attendant peace and security, is not won easily. There are many barriers and traps along the way. But the way is the speech way. We come to know who we are by knowing how we differ from others, and this means that we must talk to them. No one ever came to know himself by contemplating his silent navel. We need to identify with others to discern the discrepancies which add up to our own individuality. To find yourself you must lose yourself in others—an ancient paradox. Every time we speak to another person, seeking the identification that is so implicit in communication, we not only come to know the understandings and features and feelings we hold in common, but also those which we do not. We have to travel abroad to know what it means to be an American; we have to know a semi-saint to know the sinner side of self.

Thus, through speech we find the means to obey that ancient command of Socrates. We will find ourselves defined by the words which we speak to other people and those with which they answer, by revealing ourselves to them and having them revealed in turn to us. By knowing others we shall know ourselves. Truly this speech is a powerful magic.

4 Speech for Communication

Speech is a miracle heralded in the birthcry. Most of us succeed in performing the miracle—we learn to talk. To turn speech into communication with others, however, is something else, and though it is the silent cry of every human spirit, all too few become really good communicators. Of course we produce our Churchills and our Roosevelts, a number of perceptive parents and teachers, and even a few good quarterbacks, but most men fail to discover the language that releases their peculiar powers, which each secretly knows he has. In a lifetime few of us come to understand very many other people with deep appreciation, and the cultures of the earth look upon each other in utter consternation. Communication is not easy, and the widespread failure results in far-reaching consequences. In World War I, thirty-seven million men killed or wounded another thirty-seven million men. One generation later, the act was repeated. Then came the atomic bomb. The perspective and tone of this chapter on the nature, processes, and deterents of communication are signaled in the humorless fact that of the one hundred and eighty-five generations of man's recorded history only ten have lived in peace—according to the calculations of a Norwegian statistician.

In sharp relief, at this hour, for the first time in history, invention and economic technology promise to lift the burden of backbreaking toil from the shoulders of man. All this ingenuity is dramatized by our planes and rockets and satellites that encircle the earth. But this magnificence pales in the light that illuminates our failures as communicating creatures. We need to "Study the lines of direction of all the forces that traverse our human nature. We must study man as we have studied the stars and rocks."(1) Those were the judgments of Oliver Wendell Holmes at the turn of the century. The need is truly desperate now. The United Nations is a Tower of Babel. Wars sputter at unpredictable spots over the face of the globe, even though we know each fire may spread to a holocaust. When we turn to the domestic scene we see labor and management on constant watch, two mutually distrusting camps. The political arena from ancient time has been the place where the skills of the champion are verbal abuse, logical distortion, and emotional distress. We become so accustomed to the growls and shrill cries that we accept contemptuous and belligerent speech as a kind of foundation of civilization. But an examination of the nature of communication indicates that divisive speech is an anachronism and that civilization, what we have of it, has evolved despite a common fondness for aggressive and hostile speech.

If we shift our observation to look at the family, as an anthropologist would, we note that one out of every four couples drifts from matrimony to calumny to alimony. And the unhappy couples themselves do not understand why in the course of a few years their murmured loving speech has turned into angry commands, denials, and charges. All too few people recognize that nations grasp at each other's throats because millions upon millions of children are reared in homes where complaints and demands and dissatisfaction are the dominating qualities of the voices they hear.

We recently talked with a sixteen-year-old boy who assessed his immediate future:

> It don't look good. They [my parents] say I got to go back to that high school this fall, I can hear them now, "I don't want to hear about you being expelled again this winter. I can tell you this, we've had it. We'll put you to work where you'll damn well wish you had stayed in school!"

Despite his bitterness and distrust, the boy showed extremely quick learning when a teacher talked with him in an accepting and rewarding voice. What we are saying is that we live in a mixed-up social world from international scene to classroom to living room, but that the communications that cause the turmoil, if understood, can also remedy it. The needs for better communication are vital. This is why the word "communication" hangs uneasily on the lips of all thinking men. Let us examine the nature of communication.

The Nature of Speech Communication

Thus far in the book we have talked about speech, primarily as though it were a one-way process, as something coming out of a speaker's mouth that a cartoonist's balloon might encompass. We have largely ignored the listener—something a speaker should never do. Communication involves a sender and a receiver, and the act is understood only as we examine the field that includes both. Even the terms sender and receiver are unfortunate labels. It is true, or at least desirable, that only one of two conversants talk at one time, something children in school have a hard time learning; but even when one person is silent and listening, his face and body are constantly sending signals back to the speaker. Thus speech communication is a two-way process, not to be conceived as one where a verbal ball is being tossed back and forth, but as one where at least two, and often many, balls are being tossed in both directions at the same time. The so-called interaction of communication is a complex juggling act.

Researchers have been studying the effect in a group when the rules are altered as to who can talk and who can talk to whom.(2) Let us take a very simple case of three people and arbitrarily set up the way communication may travel. We may have five possibilities. Experimenters have studied the results in the "communication nets" shown in Figure 3.

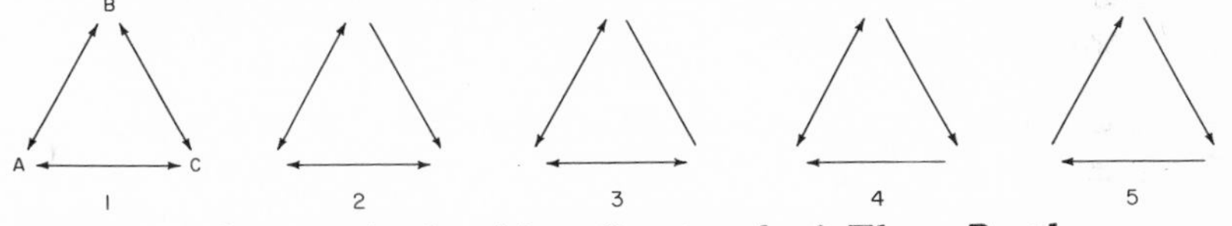

Figure 3. *Communication Nets Composed of Three People.*

The diagram in Figure 3 says more than a thousand words. Study the arrows to see who can talk and who can listen. Here are the naked conclusions indicated by the research with these nets:

1. Condition 1 solves a problem with the greatest accuracy.
2. Condition 5 solves the problem least accurately.
3. Condition 5 gets a message through in the shortest time.

4. Receivers are more confident of themselves in the two-way means of communication.
5. Senders are more sure of themselves in the one-way means of communication.
6. The morale in condition 1 is likely to be the highest.
7. Creativity is likely to be greatest in condition 1.
8. Condition 1 is the noisiest and least orderly.

Striking things may be seen about the structure of groups by noting what happens when a chain of command is established. The diagrams in Figure 4 indicate several different arrangements, all of which involve two-way communication:

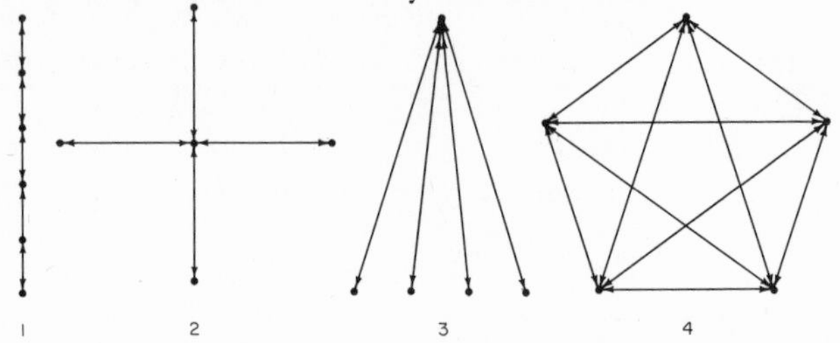

FIGURE 4. *Communication Nets Involving a Chain of Command.*

It is obvious that organization number 1 protects the man at the top from the responses of all but one man, but the chances for accurate communication throughout the system are slight indeed. This is comparable to the arrangement on board a naval vessel where error, however, is reduced to a minimum by the simple expedient of having the man who executes orders repeat them word for word to the superior who barks them.

Arrangement 3 is obviously the fastest way to shout information to all subordinates. Arrangement 2 compromises between 1 and 3, using a John Alden, the "go between." Arrangement 4 encourages both accuracy and integration since all speakers are in direct contact with each other.

If you look for the basic meanings to be gleaned from these experiments with "communication nets," you find the obvious, which is often ignored: Everybody has a mouth and ears and everybody ought to use both if communication is to be effective.

COMMON MISUNDERSTANDINGS

There are common misunderstandings about the nature of communication that need to be laid to rest. Some people think that when they tell a listener something, they have given it to him and that he has received it. But messages are not like chunks of cheese to be given and received. They are built of that more intangible stuff—the symbol. These symbols are signals, not substances. And what we try to give to our listener—a meaning—cannot be transmitted at all. It can only be aroused. The listener must participate actively if communication is to be consummated. He must decode what has been encoded, translate what has been formulated, and in so doing, he usually transforms what has been sent into something similar yet different. Human beings are not wired like television sets, so the pictures on the listener's screen are not exactly the same as those sent, but, like the television, the listener must be turned on and tuned in if any information is to be communicated.

Perhaps the misunderstanding of all misunderstandings that makes emotionally healthy communication so difficult to achieve is the common belief that our eyes and ears tell us the truth. Doubting Thomas demanded that he be shown the nail holes in the hands. "Seeing is believing" says the human race. But experiments by the psychologist Adelbert Ames, and others, demonstrate that perception—what we see and hear and feel—is determined more by our personal needs than by the stimuli to which we respond. We ought not need to document this with scientific experiment in order to lay aside the belief that we all hear and see the same thing in the same situation. Carl Sandburg tells a story that illustrates the point.

> Drove up a newcomer in a covered wagon: "What kind of folks live around here?" "Well, stranger, what kind of folks was there in the country you come from?" "Well, they was mostly a lowdown, lying, thieving, gossiping, backbiting lot of people." "Well, I guess, stranger, that's about the kind of folks you'll find around here." And the dusty gray stranger had just about blended into the dusty gray cottonwoods in a clump on the horizon when another newcomer drove up, "What kind of folks live around here?" "Well, stranger, what kind of folks was there in the country you come from?" "Well, they was mostly a decent, hardworking, lawabiding, friendly lot of people." "Well, I guess, stranger, that's about the kind of folks you'll find around here." And the second wagon moved off and blended with the dusty gray. . . .*

The mirage of water on the desert, so common to men dying of thirst, illustrates the basic fact that when we see alike we do so not so much because of the common stimuli, but because we have

---

* From *The People, Yes* (p. 120), by Carl Sandburg. Copyright 1936 by Harcourt, Brace & World, Inc., renewed 1964 by Carl Sandburg. Reprinted by permission of the publishers.

common needs. Needs govern what we see and hear, but not wholly and independently. There is the stimulus too. Stimuli have their intensity, as do needs. The gruff command, "Get out of my way" and the more common, "Excuse me, please," will not be interpreted entirely according to the needs of the listener. A loud scream is not to be ignored and will probably be interpreted for what it is.

It follows that the more our communication deals with simple, loud, and clear stimuli, the easier it is to interpret each other accurately. References to actions in time and space seem to be the simplest. The statement "I'll see you at 8:30 this evening, at the Student Center Coffee Bar, in the corner opposite the juke box" is reasonably well understood, even by a dumb blonde. As soon as we begin talking about things we cannot experience through the senses of sight, sound, and touch, we begin to have trouble. Atoms, chemical bonds, elliptical orbits, circumferences, areas, procedures, concepts, democratic action, and religious principles are difficult to communicate. The world of the unseen and the abstract causes us considerable speaking trouble, for the speaker cannot pick up an atom as he can an orange and say "look," or pluck an elliptical orbit like a guitar and say "listen," or handle a concept as he can a golf club and say "feel." But even abstractions can be communicated, if not with precision, at least without stress, so long as the sender and the receiver can escape the illusion that they deal with the facts just as they are. The nature of perception is a problem in communication, but it is not insurmountable, if understood.

Another of the chief misunderstandings about the nature of communication results from the illusion that most of the meaning people have for each other is the work of words. It is true that words are important. Without them we could not communicate as human beings, but much of the essential message is sent by postures, gestures, and facial expressions.

To hear the nonverbal broadcast one does not listen to what the speaker says, but to the way he says it. We react to his voice, to the way he stands, to his mannerisms, and to the expressions that fleet like shadows across his face. A person tells about his feelings, motives, and conflicts in this second broadcast. The listener has to imagine himself speaking with the feelings and the actual postures of the speaker in order to be able to decode and translate the message into English.

A student was presenting to a class the view that verbal language, in the main, disguises the speaker, and that the real burden of a communication is sent in the nonverbal broadcast. This he illustrated with a story not to be forgotten. He said he was driving on a super-highway one morning at dawn, and an automobile approaching at a high speed began to sway crazily from one side of the road to the other. It eventually plunged off the road, crashed into a concrete pole which broke off and fell over the automobile, bringing it to a halt. The student stopped and ran to the man's aid. The victim was hanging out of his automobile, apparently dead, his face covered with broken windshield glass. The student began to lift the glass from the man's face and the man shook his head slowly. Without opening his eyes, he mumbled, "Give me your hand." The student took the man's hand and in a few minutes the man died. The student said, "In those moments I was told about death as no words will ever tell me."

Of course, what the dying man communicated was that in the last moments of life the important thing was to be close to another human. At this point he was not concerned about who the other person was. The other was human and that was enough. It was not important to see him or to hear him, but to touch him. "Give me your hand." One is entitled to hear many things in this communication, but it is difficult to escape the point that much of the power of the communication rests in the perfect compatability of the verbal and nonverbal communication—a man sprawled, dying, asks for another's hand.

This compatability is not always to be found. Indeed, much of the confusion in communication is the felt conflict between the two broadcasts. A boy asks a girl to go to the prom. She says, "Oh, I'm so sorry. I do wish you had asked earlier. I have made other plans that I just can't alter now. Please excuse me, I have a class in ten minutes." And the boy feels that her departure was abrupt or that she had overexpressed her disappointment or that her eyes appraised him too carefully as the words gushed. People "give themselves away" in nonverbal communication unless they have learned to monitor even their voices and faces, and then they wear expressionless masks which arouse the suspicion of the listener, and even closer inspection of the nonverbal cues.

The American psychiatrist Harry Stack Sullivan makes the point that almost all of us in our culture send conflicting messages in the two broadcasts. What we put into words is always somewhat monitored. (Even your best friends won't tell you, you know.) One does not get up in class and say, except perhaps in fun, "I'm going to give the best speech you will hear today. Indeed, I shall show you

I am a pretty exceptional fellow." But these things and a multitude of other unmentionables are thought of in the course of communication and are very often said nonverbally.

But Sullivan's point about conflicting messages goes deeper, into more troubled waters. Each of us has been penalized since childhood for revealing unacceptable attitudes and feelings such as "I don't like you," "You always make me feel stupid when I talk to you," "Why do you let your hair hang in your face?" Polite society does not allow these things to be said, so they are repressed, and they are repressed so habitually, so unconsciously, that they escape from our control. Thus our nonverbal transmitters secretly send the message. As people grow into middle life, their very faces and postures tell the unspoken thoughts and feelings that dominate their lives. A truly great artist, like Andrew Wyeth, best known perhaps for his "Christina," captures these subtle nonverbal messages and puts them on canvas.

It is little wonder that the art of understanding what a person says is so incredibly difficult to acquire. There are always the lyrics and the music, and they do not always match. Worse, part of the music is unconsciously composed. And perhaps toughest of all—no meaning can be transmitted; it can only be aroused.

The Basic Processes in Communication: Identification

The most basic process in communication is that which we shall call close identification.(3) And it is probably clear from the preceding discussion that we are referring to the close identity of emotional needs. When Hitler described in vivid terms the supermen of Germany and the evil Jews that shackled the supermen, a nation marched at his heels. They understood him, not because of the facts he marshaled, for there were few, if any. They understood him because he understood their needs. Understanding is a feeling of common need. Senator McCarthy aroused the whole nation in the fifties to search out good citizens and, with subtle verbal brush strokes, gave them an ugly "pink tinge." Men perceive witches and hunt down witches quite obviously not because there are witches, but because they have a common need to hunt scapegoats. On the more positive side, men go to church and sing praises to the Almighty because they have a common need to express their aspirations and to design an image of the beautiful and the perfect and the all powerful. People come to common understanding because of common need. Research as well as common observation shows that humans come into close identification and make sense to each other basically by the commonality of their dreams and aspirations.(4) The Q-sort test, for instance, shows that friends are highly similar as far as their ideals are concerned, but no more alike than strangers in their evaluations of themselves and each other. Man identifies with man in the common needs of food, clothing, shelter, and sex, we are told, but also on the basis of his common hopes for the future.

But if identification is the magic in communication, surely speech is the magician. Two boys meet on a trout stream:

> "Catching any?" says one.
> "Couple small ones," says the other.
> "Whatcha usin'?"
> "Just a fly I made. It's a mongrel."
> "Does better than mine and I paid good money for it."
> "Where are you from?"
> "Bryon Center."
> "Gee, we play football. . . ."

And they are off. "Smith? Not any relation to Beverly Smith? . . . . I used to know a guy who went to State. . . . My uncle owns a store about ten miles east of the second crossroad south of you." The first explorations in any conversation (or public speech) are designed to find the common ground in the participants' lives if there is going to be any communication that either will listen to and both will understand. The search for common needs or appreciation is a primary function of speech.

How Identification Works

Identification is a man's most significant imaginative act. It begins in fascination. The unconscious "I wonder what it would be like to be him" is the beginning. What is the story of his past? Where does he think he is headed? Somewhere in the works of Dostoyevsky is the story of Kitty who understood the old man, though he could not speak clearly, because she always watched him and anticipated his needs. People who have been married for years often know the unexpressed thought of the other. Young lovers know what the other needs to hear. The first step in coming to understand another person is what we shall call *empathy*, whereby we escape the self and unconsciously manage to feel how the other person feels. Experiments show that a psychotherapist even takes on the heart beat and the breathing rhythm of his client. In so doing he is apparently induced to imagine the thoughts and feelings of the other person. This is what we do when we are caught up in a movie or drama. We become somebody in the story. And, likewise, this is what the actor does; he adopts the role of the person he is playing.

But the healthy person does not empty himself into others and draw his satisfaction from self-denial. To use the language of Robert Katz, (5) the person with a strong personal identity swings as a pendulum between self-identity and identity with the other person. It is this alternation between the imaginary identity with the other and the identity with the self that induces the speech of sensible communication. Many people fear swinging over into the thinking and feeling of the other person lest they lose their own identity, which turns out to be a foolish fear. It is like fearing a beautiful woman will turn ugly if you view her from another angle. To view the topic of conversation or argument from the perspective of the other person's needs is the only way any communion is going to develop between two or more people.

How may we, desiring to speak more effectively, learn to find the common emotional bonds with those we want to talk to? The answer is to be found in the ways humans share and act together. People can walk together, dance together, meet together, eat together, sing together, and not least of all, talk together. They form words, creeds, and declarations of allegiances, which they speak in unison. All the rituals men go through together—those of the fraternity and sorority not excepted—are the result of man's often unconscious knowledge that it is thus that we induce in each other the feelings that bond us. In the end it is the common language that binds people. The very fact that we use the same words, as different as their intellectual meanings may be, induces common feelings. Indeed, much of the educational process you are undergoing is an identification shift that results from learning the language of the college environment in general, and of each course in particular. Common words in common tones tend to induce common feelings—the foundation of communication.

He who would develop the art of communication may well capture a vivid image of the tread of foot, the tone of voice, the peculiar movements, and the unique phrases of the person he would like to understand. In privacy one may imitate these, not to make a spoken cartoon as the television imitator does, but to capture the feelings that induce that unique style of the person. We recall a brilliant girl who developed her powers as a speech therapist by listening over and over again to the recordings of clients and echoing them almost in unison. To understand another is to feel how it feels to speak as he speaks.

The Translation Process

The intellectual counterpart of close identification is the translation process, the re-encoding of the language of the other into one's own silent self-talk. To memorize another's speech, as we do in the declamation or the interpretative reading, may induce something akin to the feelings of the author, and we may speak with pretended rapture. But we do not know what we are saying, we do not have an intellectual grasp, unless we also, at least unconsciously, paraphrase the message into our own words.

We recall overhearing an elderly lady at the close of a philosophical lecture exclaim, "Wonderful, wonderful." "What did he say?" asked her companion. "Oh, I haven't the slightest idea," she said. "And I know that sounds strange. But I loved his elegant language." This woman had obviously enjoyed the music of sophisticated speech, and she had identified closely with the speaker. But she did not know what he had said because she did not, and probably could not, translate his words into her own self-talk.

Here is an example of the statement of one person and its translation by another:

Speaker: I have very serious doubts about the use of examinations.
Listener: (*To himself*) He does not believe in final examinations.

The listener could have translated: "We ought to use exams differently than we do. . . . I wonder how," or "We put too much stock in what exams show," or "We ought to use more tests," or many other ways, which will help him understand the speaker as he proceeds. Right or wrong in his judgment, the listener must translate, he must constantly recode if he is to understand.

The sophistication of the translation process and the miracle of learning it stands out in bold relief when we examine the humorous translations that result when children are operating at something near the mockingbird level: "A vacuum," said one child "is the place the Pope lives." And one little scientist observed that "The earth is a vacillating object that makes one resolution every twenty-four hours." Another child in answer to the question "where do the Indians go when they die?" answered, "Way down yonder in the cornfield." These stories highlight the unconscious translation process that goes on all the time we communicate.

How Translation Works

How does the process work? Each man's self-talk, as he listens, is a re-encoding process, and all the foregoing discussion suggests that the re-encoded message is, of necessity, a transformed message. People never say "the same thing in different words." Meaning is something woven into the peculiar associations of the words in a statement. And meaning is always an active formulating process. The only task the words of the other person do is call up words (or some other symbols) which the listener formulates into a pattern that makes sense to his needs.

Thus—and this is important—the person who seeks to be understood by others expects to hear the thoughts and feelings he arouses in them, not a parroting of his own words. If one of two conversants should say "I think I'll drop out of school at the end of the semester," his companion is not likely to say, in an effort to indicate he understands, "You think you'll drop out of school at the end of the semester." (The unhappy student is trying to escape his echo chamber, not increase its intensity by listening to his own speech repeated.) Even if the nonverbal speech indicated the companion is in tune, this mirror statement would say, "Did you hear what you said?" If the statement is said out of tune, as when it is intended to hurt the other, it becomes something like a child's irritating chant: "I think I'll drop out of school. I think I'll drop out of school." When we cause a person to feel the deep satisfaction that he really was heard, we say not his words, but instead a statement of our own which reflects his meaning—and is sensitive to his feelings. "You mean you are going to drop out for good?" or better, "I guess you have had it for awhile." The first speaker now knows that he has crashed through and that his feelings and message made their impact on his companion.

The reader may ask, "Does the same kind of translation go

on when we 'transmit' information?" And the answer is "Yes." There is no other recourse. If a person says the simple statement, "This is a pencil," the listener registers silently, "Yes, I get it, that is a pencil." The translation process here seems almost parrot talk. This is the kind of almost verbatim translation that goes on when children are going through that "What is it?" stage that plagues a parent. Most speech, however, does not label things but the combination of things, our feelings, and our thoughts, and sometimes all three. Then the translation process is difficult and complex. Assume you received the following examination question. "What is meant by the statement: 'In order to mature a person needs freedom'?" You would know better than to answer: "The statement means just what it says: 'In order to mature a person needs freedom.'" You know that what the statement really calls for is a series of other statements, each one of which serves as a part of the fence that bounds the territory referred to in the statement to be discussed. Here is one of the translations you might give: "If a person is going to grow up he has to learn how to make decisions for himself. But one cannot make decisions if he does not have the freedom of choice. . . . Therefore, freedom to make personal decisions, even bad ones—in the judgment of others—is necessary. . . ." As you proceed you would include translations of your own statements such as: "That does not mean that anybody can do just what he pleases, in other words . . . let me give an example . . . some people would say . . . on the other hand . . . in short. . . . Yet . . . in addition . . . this is my point. . . ." Our language and our common practice of trying every tack indicates that at least unconsciously we know that the communication of any complex piece of information is a game of charades, where the communicator tries many indirect means that say in sum: Somewhere within the bounds of these statements you will find language for your own thought that will not be too far afield of what I am trying to say to you.

If we want to be understood very clearly we are particularly careful to work very close to the language of the other person. Sometimes, however, we just want to stir the mental processes of the other. Then we do not pin ideas down with many careful illustrations. We thus excite the other person to help us design a common thought. "How about this . . . ? Hey, I got an idea . . . or maybe what you mean. . . ." are the initial rejoinders of a person excited to think creatively when the boundaries of translation are not too strictly drawn.

For perfect comprehension of the other person, of course, the perfect translation would come from identical experiences coded in identical words by identical twins. In such a case, which never happens, the person who heard the comment would restate it. We approximate this when we deal with reference to objects and actions in time and space. "Please bring your texts to class tomorrow" may be translated "I shall have to remember to bring my *text* tomorrow. Did he say *texts*? I said text. Huh?" Then the student asks "You mean both our speech text and the anthology of readings?" By the translation process, comparing the words heard and our own response words, we determine the points of likeness and difference and check out the differences and doubtful spots by our next comments—easily done when we deal with time and space references.

This all seems so obvious we tend to dismiss its significance for our lives. Yet, how many times do we try to say something we think we understand and find it is not there? Students sometimes speak up in class and become exasperated because nobody understands. Speech students often come to the instructor after a speech and explain their disappointment. "I prepared well. I thought I had a good speech." Often they will ask, "What happened?" Many students who study diligently fail examinations. They commonly say, "I thought I knew the material."

Though the student does not know it, these reports indicate that he has not learned how to translate adequately, that he has depended upon a feeling of familiarity with the language of the other, but that he has not tested out the symbols with which he grasped the feeling of comprehension. That feeling may be little other than a sense of false confidence.

Students, not recognizing the importance of the translation process, often spend useless energy underlining long passages in their texts. If not done too extensively, this practice does provide an outline for review, but it would be much better if they would write in the margin their own statements of the important ideas to remember. We knew an elderly man who spent much of his old age on the porch, propped in a chair, reading the Scriptures. Each time he read a verse he put a dot in the margin with a different colored pencil, indicating to the Lord, who obviously is not too busy to keep such tabulations, how often he had been through the Good Book. As we recall, the old gentleman did not improve in his understanding, diligent as he was.

In the process of this writing, your authors have become highly sensitive to the role of translation. Each of these chapters has been revised many times, searching not so much for the ideas, but for the language which would be translatable. Each time one of us finished a chapter he expressed confidence that he had said it clearly and in final form, only to have his co-author later rewrite sentences and cut whole sections because he could not understand them. In turn, by comparing translations the writer would often discover still different patterns of language for his thought. In this winnowing process, we have done consciously and laboriously what people in conversations over coffee cups or backyard fences do every day, sometimes well, sometimes poorly. We spend our lives translating.

Probably the failures of most of us to find language that can be easily translated is our tendency to ignore the language we have used when people listened to us attentively. We get too much absorbed in our own self-talk and test out too little its impact on others. When the points we state are rejected we unfortunately try to ram them home. "Sure you would lie down and let the Commies walk all over you. Me, I would draw the line right there and the first. . . ." In these kinds of conversations, and they ring through the night in a thousand dormitories, we develop gradually and sometimes painfully our ability to get translated accurately, which we achieve not by repeating those precious words that seem to encase the truth for us, but by searching out those words that make sense to our conversant.

No greater value is offered to you in your speech course than additional opportunities to phrase your most precious thoughts in language which makes sense to others. And you miss a bet if you do not try to restate your best thoughts in as many ways as you can, always alert to the language that others respond to; to restate the language of others, so that by their approval you know you have captured their feeling and thought; and to restate again and again in your own words the thoughts of good speakers, so that you may learn to speak with appreciation, pertinence, and the power of precision.

Coexistence is the central theme of the latter half of the twentieth century, and survival of the race depends upon people learning how to accommodate their language to those who find it difficult to understand them. The discovery of sane language—translations that satisfy the speaker's needs and make good sense to the listener—is still a lagging art. Most of us marvel and quote the few men who have developed the talent. What manner of man is this, we say to ourselves, who puts the words in my ear I would I had formed on my tongue?

Here is a sample of a child's private self-talk that she is trying so hard to put into communicative speech:

> We had a fight at the bridge. Well, uh, Peggy and Amy and Lynda and I. Over (gulp) Peggy was just Peggy said, "I'm going home because you guys aren't very nice," and so then Lynda went home and then—no first Lynda went home and then Peggy went home and Lynda went and then I went to get my bike, mad ya know (gulp) then I started out first and then Peggy passed me and then I went home and everyone beated me home 'cept Amy wouldn't leave me alone so I was walking my bike up a hill and, small steps you know 'cause I was mad and then Amy came in the driveway ahead of me and she said (gulp) come here Penny or do you want me to come down there and so I said just go on with the rest of them, you probably don't like me any more either.

Her mother said, "You had a fight?" and the child coming into close identification with her mother and her language translated her above self-talk into:

> We had a fight at the bridge just because Peggy said we weren't nice. So we started home and they all beat me. Then Amy wanted to play with me but I just told her to go on because she probably didn't like me either.

We may smile, but at each stage in our maturation each of us is faced with the challenge of trying to translate his new-found awareness into language that speaks to his fellow men.

Messages—the Objective Information

Textbooks in speech, since the time of the Greeks, have dealt in detail with the basic principles of the art of casting thought in language that is easily translated by the listener. We should probably not spade that garden again. But it does seem wise to fit the message into its appropriate place in the description of communication.

Two things especially facilitate listening. The first is clarity. And the cardinal principle in clarity is simplicity. We are told that the atomic bombs were dropped on Japan in 1945 because the Japanese answer to the warning and demand for surrender was not interpreted as intended. With tolerance for the great differences in the two languages, a clear "Yes" or "No" would not have been misunderstood. Messages need to be simple; to use a more pleasant example, if one wants to say, "Hydrochloric acid harms drain pipes" it is not very helpful to say, "The efficiency of hydrochloric acid is indisputable, but the corrosive residue is incompatible with metallic permanance." It is much more clear, if less elegant, to say, "Hydrochloric acid eats the hell out of drain pipes." Often college students, and even some professors, feel they exercise their intellectual powers if they decorate their speech with bouquets of prestigious words. But the truth is that the use of simple words lets one know whether the speaker has anything to say and offers a certain guarantee if he does, that it will be understood. Lincoln managed to talk simply.

Perhaps the central factor in simplicity, other than the choice of simple words, is simple organization. Human thinking is a tangle of associations. And if a person is interested enough in the speaker or his topic, he can untangle almost any jumble of words in seeking the sense. Psychiatrists spend their lives doing it, but most of us do so with reluctance and only when strongly motivated. Thus, one of the major emphases in a speech text concerns the organization of speeches, and the first principle of organization though elementary, should be taken seriously. It is this: first, tell the audience "what you want to tell them," the conclusion of your thinking, so they may know what to expect; second, explain the material that causes you to conclude that way; and finally, tell them the conclusion again. Thus, listeners know what you are trying to say. They can compare your arguments with your conclusions. They see the structure all along. The usual text elaborates this by suggesting kinds of outlines, offering examples, showing how to develop introductions, evidence, transitions, and conclusions. But the basic rule is simple and hinges on the fact that a statement makes sense only when we know what it is related to.

Besides starting "with the point" and keeping it in focus, a second cardinal principle in organization is simple repetition. Repetition is the cement that binds words together into a structure. One may test this assertion by the following procedure. Count the repetitions of the nouns, adjectives, adverbs, and verbs of an article or speech, and you will find that the three or four most commonly used words form a telegraphic-like statement of the central idea of the article. Advertisers know this well. And every discerning speaker or writer, who occasionally inserts a statement like, "But my main point is . . ." is repeating the key words of the code, for he knows the listener may otherwise be lost in a sea of words. He says, "Now hear this, now hear this," like the navy boatswain who sounds off with the orders of the day.

The very language structure itself is highly repetitive. The linguists call this "redundancy." Studies have shown that, as a result of the redundancy in the language, people can miss as much as 45 per cent of a message and still get the gist. Mathematicians say that English is 50 per cent redundant and that if it were less so one could not make crossword puzzles. The Lord may have had in mind the weary commuter on the suburban train when he built redundancy into the language. In any event, if the redundancy in a speech is adequate and interesting enough not to bore, the listener has time to open his mental dictionary and to translate.

Information Input Overload

The point of the above discussion is lost if the speaker, though clear and orderly, gives too much information. Listeners can carry only so much current before they blow a fuse. Many student speakers, not knowing this, crowd too many ideas into a speech. A test after a speech indicates that only a few things can be stored. The admonition, "Do not give too much information," is especially pertinent for three- to ten-minute speeches. One student tried to explain the details of genetic mutation in a five-minute speech. Listeners became exasperated, and the speaker wrongly and unhappily interpreted frustration as rejection. This does not mean speeches should be superficial. One may plunge into a deep pool for a three-minute dip, but he need not try to swim the Hellespont.

Dr. James G. Miller, Director of the Mental Health Research Institute at Ann Arbor, is devoting his energies to an exploration of the way the human nervous system handles a deluge of information. He has found that the human adjusts in one or more of the following seven ways:

1. *Omission.* One just does not hear point 22, or if he does, he does not write it down in his notes.
2. *Error.* He writes down $E = M^2c$ instead of $E = mc^2$.
3. *Queuing.* He writes one thing as he listens to something else, hoping all the time the speaker will cough or choke or forget what he was going to say, until the pen catches up with the mouth.

4. *Filtering.* This is very much like omission, but different in technique. The listener establishes categories for determining what to listen to. Perhaps he listens only to the speaker's funny stories and pays no attention to the points they illustrate. Or he counts the number of times the speaker says "ramifications," or notes the way he whistles his *s*'s. What one filters out may make good material for imitations at the fraternity house and bad material for examination day.
5. *Approximation.* The listener gets only a general idea of what the speaker said, "It went something like this. . . ." The listener does not make errors; he just bogs down in vagaries.
6. *Multiple channels.* The listener increases his capacity by watching the mannerisms of the speaker and listening for the meanings in his voice. Seeing and hearing supplement each other.
7. *Escape.* If decoding becomes too exasperating the listener finally shuts off his "hearing aid" and lapses into thinking about the next class or last night's date.(6)

One of the first things a speaker should aim to learn is how to judge the amount of information his audience can tolerate. This he should not exceed. The temptation to say too much is great because we live in a day of the information explosion. Millions of men in the industrial, governmental, and educational laboratories of the earth work late into the night, and the printing presses run day and night. You, as an information receiver, must often cry out against the lecturer who packs in too much. He is a bad model, and you should not follow his example.

Metaphor

The metaphor is the primary language tool in communication because it works with images that the listener is almost sure to be able to translate into his self-talk. By definition a metaphor means "a carry over," a "transfer." The metaphor is a translating device that recognizes the fact, as cited earlier, that the easiest meanings to translate are those that have references in time and space. "Write your name in the upper right-hand corner of the paper, now" is instantaneously translatable. "The iron curtain," "a Mickey Mouse," "that's the way the ball bounces," "a push-over," "a brain," "an apple polisher," "all shook up," and all the language that "catches on" has that specific reference to some sensory experience which makes it immediately translatable.

The metaphor is a shortened illustration. When we get into trouble trying to find the words that say something, we almost unconsciously say, "Now let me illustrate. It's like this . . ." and we make a comparison, an analogy. Note the illustration that holds the following discussion intact.

> In this discussion of information, the thing that gets translated may be thought of as a ball that gets tossed back and forth between communicators. But that is not quite it either, because as we have said earlier, the listener never catches the thing the speaker threw, but something like it. The game of communication is played with a soft clay or plasticene ball that changes shape to conform to the hands of the person who catches it.

Note that the illustration is composed of many metaphors that fit the ball-game illustration—the hands for brain, the ball for information, the catching for listening. An illustration is an extended metaphor.

The importance of learning to use language that fits the senses is well dramatized by the exasperated person who, failing in an act of communication, cries out, "What do you want me to do—draw you a picture?" The answer is "Yes." And the more sophisticated people become, the more necessary it is for them to know how to draw pictures. Self-talk becomes more and more private as we gradually grow to become unique and mature. C. P. Snow, the British novelist and scientist, has created a considerable stir in recent years with his book about the dangerous language differences between the political and scientific worlds.(7) Any group—including that of the largest group, the culture—founders in turbulent waters when the captain and the first mate speak different tongues.

The chemist pricks up his ears when he hears the term "unstable element"; the philosopher, when he hears reference to the "logical positivists"; and the college student, when he hears the lovely voice of Lulu Belle. No task is more important to the would-be speaker than his constant search for the language that speaks to all men, and he will find reward when his search is for the vivid word. The student speaker should monitor his tongue, and when the audience sends signals that indicate interest and acceptance, he may well stop and examine the words and ideas with them. He should store away what he learns at this point, to call forth at a future hour when he is lost talking to himself. Former British Prime Minister Clement Atlee once said, "The people of the world are islands shouting to each other over seas of misunderstanding." A large part of the problem of any man who cannot be understood is that he cannot find the metaphor that his listeners can translate.

Midway Oasis

Thus far we have discussed the peculiar nature of communication and how it works. Information, the thing that gets communicated, is induced by the processes of identification and translation. We have tried to make clear that we humans perceive according to our needs, that the feeling that we understand each other is a feeling of common or conflicting needs, and that we interpret the message of the other person as we interpret his needs. In short, the information that passes the boundary between two people will be shaped by the kinds of emotion each arouses in the other. The key to understanding is close identification; what is understood is always a translation.

The formula that telegraphs our view of communication may be presented thus:

Information * = Emotional identification + intellectual translation
(* what is said – the repetition)

The formula is simple; the art of making the formula work is not and is indeed man's greatest challenge.

Deterrents to Communication

The enemies of communication, the deterrents, are also simple to understand and difficult to correct. The enemies of communication, and thus the enemies of the human race, are noise, distance, time lag, and the increasing size of the group trying to communicate. Let us discuss them.

External Noise

Noise is a popular term used today for the things that garble a message. In slightly more technical language, noise refers to all the disruptive factors that get into a communication channel and make it difficult for the listener to translate the message as intended by the speaker. Carpenters hammering in a hall during a speech, students whispering in the back row, wind rattling the windows, a pretty girl in the second row just sitting there, the football player in the back row jiggling his foot, all these are technically noise in the communication circuit. Any kind of disturbance that interrupts attention to the intended source of a message is noise. Noise of any description is bad for communication. One need not labor the importance of a noise-free radio channel for the pilot landing a jet.

Internal Interference With Communication

A noisy noise annoys an oyster. It also annoys a man, and it should be clear by this point that anxiety is the noisiest noise in all human communication. People who cannot accept each other—and their name is legion—are certain to fear each other. The mass of men huddle together in highly restrictive groups to mask the silent screams within themselves, in the buzz of meaningless conversation. The cynics intepret the burden of distrust and resulting communicative eruptions in our social world as evidence of the evil basic to man. We do not share this hopeless faith. We see no point in teaching or learning speech if man is basically corrupt. This book rests on the conviction that verbal patterns are learned patterns. We find the source of the evil that pervades our language in the obvious economic conflicts of supply and demand. To use Bertrand Russell's figure, the fruits of the plum tree have not yet filled the bellies of all men. Men will be anxious and will be inclined to attack each other until hunger is eradicated. For the first time in history the human race is within reach of techiques to produce a sufficient supply of food, but there are other hungers.

And now we must learn fast that men with their barns filled can be anxious still and that many anxieties are caused by the language—verbal and nonverbal—that people use when they talk to each other about each other. Nobody escapes this terrible power. It is interesting to note that even our Presidents, with all the proof of their social acceptance, are deeply burned by the criticism they read in the papers. And these words are not even said in person. Note the help or hindrance written in the judgment scrawled on the faces of your listeners when you speak in class.

Anxiety is the signal that self-esteem is threatened. Carl Rogers suggests that the state of tension of our world reflects the hazards of the social world. Since survival is basic, as Abraham Maslow points out, safety comes first in the human value scheme; where anxiety is pronounced it dominates. Harry Stack Sullivan makes the crucial point that anxiety is the destructive commonplace of society.(8) Anxiety is like the common cold. It leads to all sorts of other problems, and is so prevalent that we tend to accept it as normal. Anxiety shouts, but it often is not heard by the external ear, though its vibrations are felt throughout the self, grievously disrupting the identification and translation processes.

The overall effect of anxiety upon most people, especially those who try to repress it, is to make them conform, to cause them to lean upon the words of other people for security. It causes them to huddle into tightly knit groups that chant common words and to fly at the throats of those who speak words they do not understand. The total effect of anxiety is rigidity and resistance to new messages.(9)

Research in industry on the flow of communication up and down the chain of command tells about the distorting effects of anxiety.(10) Speech flows downward more readily than upward for words like water have their weight. The authority structure tends to put anxious meaning into words which trouble both the speaker and the listener. Men above in command say they solicit the ideas of men below. Men below say, "No, they don't." Men above feel that they inform men below. Men below say, "No, they don't." Men above in a chain of command report that they understand their subordinates, but that their own superiors do not seem to understand them very well. Men in top management tend to feel the major motive of the production worker is more money. Workers at the bottom feel they are more motivated by the drive for security. Men at the top tend to underestimate the common workers need to get along well with his fellow workers, according to reports from the Institute for Social Research at Ann Arbor. Anxiety twists the meaning of words.

May we be so bold as to examine the communication between instructors and students? Quite frankly the educational system inherits an authoritarian structure, designed to bring students to terms. We have all been raised under the whip of tests and grades, and anxiety eats away at the learning process in almost all classrooms. Not a little of the student's speech difficulty may be attributed to an institutional structure designed more in the interest of compliance than of learning. Saying these things here will not eradicate them, but if one can understand them it may help him to gain better control of his speech powers.

There is also a certain advantage to be gained from the tensions aroused by the classroom speech situation. All public speaking is anxiety arousing, for public speaking is really an arrogant act. "Ladies and gentlemen, lend me your ears"—and your minds (the core of your being) and your time (the only thing you really own—which slips away with each tick of the clock). Most men scrutinize a speaker with a critical eye when he asks them to lend him their ears, and rightly so. Almost all public speech situations are fear arousing. The fear arousal inherent in the speech class does offer, then, an opportunity to toughen up oneself for the public speaking situation.

But let not this truth obscure the greater truth that anxiety corrupts normal human relationships. Such speech as the following: "I don't know what you are coming to," "I want my money; I wouldn't work here another hour," "God knows I hate her now," "We shall negotiate, but only from a position of strength," when traced to their sources come to the poisoned waters of the twin springs of anxiety and belligerence. The union of the two and their relation to speech is expressed vividly in Sarett and Foster's long-accepted basic principle: "Effective speech is unobtrusive and therefore disarming."

Somehow we must learn to lower the anxiety in the speech of men, to truly disarm speech. The first step is to throw away the worn-out value attached to militant speech. Strangely, this admonition gets twisted and associated with sentimentality and weakness. The all too common belief that courageous men speak firmly and make the cowards quake needs close scrutiny. It is true, some cowards do quake, but then some do not. They belch their anxieties and humorlessly blame the unpleasant sound on others. Courageous speech asks no man to quake. Some day we must surely come to see the significance of the accumulating evidence that the brain waves of chronically anxious people have the brain-wave characteristics of brain-injured people.(11)

Anxiety fouls up the identification process. It prevents the sender from coding his message appropriately. It prevents the listener from interpreting the message accurately.

Distance

There are other factors, almost wholly physical in character, which get in the way of communication. Let us examine the facts about distance between communicators.

One study shows that friendship varies, even within the short span of 180 feet.(12) The closer people are in physical contact, the more they talk. And the more they talk the more likely they will weld together. Distance is an enemy of communications. Absence, the old saw to the contrary, makes the heart grow harder. It is because of this that the ancient political philosophers declared that a governmental structure should grow no larger than the distance a man can cast his voice. But men have been ingenious in stretching that distance. Bullhorns, drums, messengers, and the written documents that were invented thousands of years ago defy the limitation of the lungs. The invention of the printing press has had a strange inverse effect, muffling the command of priest and monarch, and in turn giving voice to the thoughts of common men, who now could read for themselves. Thus, the Reformation and the Enlightenment. Then came the telegraph and telephone. A new age was born with the invention of radio and television. A single voice and a man's face can now be instantly heard and seen around the earth. These inventions and the aircraft have made one loosely knit confederation of the world. The communication barrier of physical distance has fallen. Space, in itself alone, is no longer a deterrent to communication. The astronauts, encircling the earth, can talk to their wives and children at home.

Time

The time factor gives more difficulty. Indeed, man's earliest efforts to conquer space sometimes lengthened the time involved in sending and receiving messages (letters and manuscripts, for instance). But smoke signals and drums extended the voice of man without distressing delay in time. The great electronic inventions in communication, radio, radar, telegraph, telephone, television, and telawoman—who in strict truth is electronic only in the sense that she is electrifying—have conquered not only space but time. Radio and television have eliminated the time factor for one-way communication, as books and letters have not. Actually radio and television are limited instruments for communication, in large measure because they do not permit instantaneous feedback to the sender. No mass media does.

Size of Population

A student may go to college in New York and talk to his parents in California. His great-grandfather could not have done that. This simple fact creates the illusion that conquering communicative space and time diminishes communication problems. The converse is true, for the result is an increase in the number of people involved. If we double the distance, density of population remaining constant, we quadruple the number of people who get into the "conversation." If we triple the distance we add nine times as many people, and on it goes at this accelerating rate. For some strange reason many people believe that the larger the communication system the better the communication—"If it's big, it's gotta be good," so the reasoning goes. But James G. Miller, referred to earlier, has demonstrated that just the converse is true. A simple cell handles its information more efficiently than a multicelled organ of the body, such as the heart. The heart in turn is more efficient than the entire coordinated body. One person is a more efficient communication system than are two. The larger the company or university or nation, the longer it takes to get a message through and effect a real change. The very increase in the number of voices results in a kind of cultural noise like the rumble of a city. The machine loses its power to send messages back to the head; the identification process ceases to function; translation becomes garbled.(13)

Some of the dynamics involved can be seen by examining the behavior of small groups. In groups of two to seven people, identification and translation are relatively easy, and there is little need for group rules. Each person who speaks is in turn the leader, and the leadership can pass quite unofficially from one to the other. With group membership above six or seven, things begin to change. The structure of the group becomes more formal. Somebody has to be the "boss," someone has to decide what the group is going to talk about and who is going to talk. Some people begin to talk more and some less as a group increases its membership. Subgroups begin to develop unless a commanding voice dominates attention. In groups ranging from seven to twelve in membership, a skillful leader can induce discussion. As soon as the group increases to fifteen and twenty and more, group discussion is done. The leader and three or four "panelists" do the talking, much as if they belonged to a group of seven or under, and the rest sit and listen. The notion that discussion groups (or classes) of twenty and twenty-five can interact like small, informal groups is pure fantasy. It does not work because the very size brings out the speaker in some and the listener in others. Moreover, when too many talk the variety of views becomes so confusing that only a genius at generalization can see how all the views fit together and make sense.

Another way of looking at group size throws considerable light on the problem of the college student in the dormitory. Research indicates that two people form an extremely unstable group.(14) They must identify and translate or their communication weaknesses and failures become intolerably apparent. Thus the speech between two is usually highly emotional and tense. Disagreement must be avoided if at all possible. On the other hand, if disagreement is avoided, the opportunity for identification and translation is simpler than with any larger number, and thus the possibility for information exchange is at its maximum.

A group of three is highly stable, for majority control is easily established.(15) If, however, three-way identification cannot be established, three roommates can create an unhappy situation. All too often one is an outsider. Three is a crowd. If the group is unstable the coalition keeps changing, and this is an unhappy situation too, for none of the three knows who will be out tomorrow.

A group of five seems in many ways the most satisfactory, from an emotional point of view. It provides easy emotional relationships within. If three identify, usually the other two, under the circumstances, will find each other mutually agreeable. The odd number provides stability and eliminates power deadlocks, as exist potentially in groups of two and four. Five provides enough variety for stimulation, and opportunity for easy participation by all. As already indicated, six and seven begin to reach the maximum size if a group is to function without formal structure—a boss man and some rules.

The smaller the group the greater the tension and the greater the necessity for agreement.(16) As groups grow larger people feel more free to disagree, perhaps because they will usually be joined by other dissenters. As the population of a group grows larger, interaction, the urge to power, and the need to laugh increase. The reader may decide for himself the reasons for these peculiarities of the human race.

Man has found a number of ways to attack the communication barriers of distance and time. Perhaps there are no solutions for the communication problems of population size. No one yet has found a way to stop the wind or still the waves of the sea.

Summary and Conclusion

Throughout this chapter we have been trying to make clear the nature of communication, how it works, and the things that disturb the process. In summary, one may see the interrelationships of the working parts in the following formula:

$$\frac{\text{Amount of Information}}{(\text{Amount said} - \text{Repetitions})} = \frac{\text{Identification} + \text{Translation}}{\text{Noise} + \text{Space} + \text{Time} + \text{Population Size}}$$

Man, the brain animal, is driven by survival need to absorb a constant flow of information, much as he does food. Sensory deprivation experiments dramatically demonstrate this. For several hours after the person is returned to normal sight, sound, and feeling, his sensory mechanism, particularly his vision, does not operate correctly, and he talks drunkenly and often incoherently. A fish cannot live for long out of water, and man cannot live, at least rationally, outside his sea of symbols.

The quality of the symbols we employ, especially the verbal symbols, is desperately important. We wish we might close this discussion in more victorious tones, for we do not wish to dampen the spirit of youth. But the simple truth is that good communication is still the achievement of the minority and the need for communication improvement throughout the mass of men is the challenge of our age. Surely the college student of this hour knows that he faces an uncertain future in an uncertain world and that he among many must learn to relate to others in such fashion as to pass more accurate information than has been our custom. The student who will be of aid in the troubled years ahead will examine his communication with careful scrutiny and will make good communication one of the prime goals of his life.

We are still immensely ignorant about the communication process. Granted this, we already know much more than common practice would suggest. And indeed, no amount of new information will improve the communication among men until they come to place a salutary value on the power to tune in on each other and to translate the self-talk of each into that of the other. Human future hinges on this learning.

Control Speech

5

Speech is also a power tool. We use it daily to manipulate others, to bend them to our will. In this sense it is a truly magical act. The baby learns this early. He cries "Mama" and lo, she appears, almost as though he had rubbed Aladdin's lamp and said abracadabra. "Gimme cookie," he says, and often it is forthcoming. Speech is a tool. We adults have talked so much so long that it is difficult indeed for us to appreciate this particular magical power that speech provides, though we use it for this purpose constantly. The mouth can reach beyond the arms, but until the child discovers this important fact he speaks very little.

Throughout our lives we use our speech to amplify our own small potencies by getting others to fulfill our needs. Coaxing, wheedling, cajoling, requesting, nagging, persuading, we find our strength multiplied. Each of us acquires the feelings of a giant when we learn that we can use our speech to order, direct, and command others to do our bidding. A child's first word is often not a noun that names something, but a command: "Out!" "Up!" "Milk!" (1) Even "Mama!" can be a command. Indeed, the child first seems to sense his own individuality in the hour when he learns to say "No!" As Joseph Conrad says in his novel *Lord Jim*, "There is a weird power in a spoken word."

Most of us do not realize how often we use speech for control.

Very rarely can two people do anything together without one or the other using some of this magical power. Skinner, the famous psychologist, divides all speaking into two categories: *tacts* and *mands*. Tacts are statements; mands are utterances used to control. He shows clearly that the inherent utility of mand speech is due to the reinforcement it receives:

> *Wait!* is followed by someone's waiting and *Sh-h!* by silence. Much of the verbal behavior of young children is of this sort. *Candy!* is characteristically followed by the receipt of candy and *Out!* by the opening of a door.*

Any behavior which gets such reinforcement is likely to appeal, and so much of our verbal lives is spent requesting, demanding, advising, and directing others.

We also use mand speech in controlling ourselves to a degree which is surprising. Much of this is silent, but a little introspection will indicate its prevalence. It is obvious that the still small voice of conscience speaks in mands, but even much of our voluntary behavior has a similar expression. We even direct ourselves to pick up that pencil or to get a hamburger. There is a curious disorder called *apraxia* resulting from brain damage in which the person may not be able voluntarily to protrude his tongue because he cannot find the internal words to command the action, though he may use his tongue to lick some peanut butter from his upper lip. We are not usually conscious of these inner commands that control our behavior, but they are always present.

We often meet persons who find it difficult to accept the responsibility for making decisions, who procrastinate, who chronically hesitate, or who seem incapable of leading others. And there are those who rebel unreasoningly against all demands, no matter how carefully phrased. Often the histories of these individuals reveal that they have been subjected in early childhood to more command speech than any child should have to endure or that they have suffered too many demands accompanied by threat or extreme punishment. If mand speech becomes horribly unpleasant we cannot bear to put it into our own mouths even to control ourselves. The race of tomorrow will know much more about the importance of mand speech in the education of its offspring.

---

* From *Verbal Behavior* (p. 35), by B. F. Skinner. Copyright 1957 by Appleton-Century-Crofts, Inc. Reprinted by permission of Appleton-Century-Crofts.

The power can be used for good or ill. When used appropriately, speech serves as the indispensable instrument of all human cooperation. We need this magnificent power to organize a group, to mobilize the energies of all the individuals within it toward a common goal. They must be persuaded to join together; they must be directed. Without speech, we would be helpless to undertake not only the conquest of space, but even the ordinary pursuits of existence. Even a pencil is the product of a hundred commands.

Our society requires that each of its members belong not only to one group but to many. We work and play and live cooperatively. Each of us will find opportunities for leadership where we can exercise our speech for control. There will be times when we must accept the follower role, but our cultural need for status makes a strong force for impelling us often to take charge and direct our co-workers. In large measure these highly rewarded leadership roles require some real facility in the use of persuasion and command.

Fortunately, all of us get some real training in the use of control speech. From earliest childhood we are exposed to the directions and commands of our parents and associates. "Do this! Do that! Don't!" The models are always in our ears. Since much of our early learning is by identification, we may—if those models of command speech are often accompanied by angry tones—find ourselves years later unconsciously speaking harshly even in such an utterance as "Please pass the salt." If a parent will listen to his child at play, commanding his dolls and toys to his bidding, he may hear the mood of his own control speech. We hope that it will not sound harsh for, as we shall see later, we need not always use threat to gain compliance; we may also use the persuasion of appeal. Indeed, our culture puts a premium on the latter and teaches its bosses to give their orders in such a manner that the threat is hidden rather than obvious, even when it is present. Weapons may be carried. They must not be brandished.

One can scarcely examine the speech of control without asking questions about the nature of leadership and its role in the social process. What do we know about leaders and leadership?

Characteristics of the Leader

The leader is a speaker, and if he is the spearhead of change he must have "high sending power." Studies show that the men of a group who emerge as leaders express more thought units per hour than nonleaders do.(2) They simply talk more. They tend to have more positive attitudes toward themselves than the average person, and they usually feel comfortable about the effect of others on themselves. Perhaps one might say they feel good about the overall effect of the give-and-take of verbal interaction. Almost paradoxically, they are inclined to feel that the world has not been particularly good to them, which probably accounts for their urge to speak up and take charge. Leaders tend to be verbal about what can be achieved and about their capacity to do the job. Leaders rank high in the need to make their views known. "Vanity," said Napoleon, "made the Revolution; liberty was only a pretext."

According to research, leadership ability shows a positive, but low, correlation with size, weight, appearance, intelligence, self-assurance, friendliness, determination, and energy, which suggests, says Sanford, that perhaps leadership is itself a separate trait.(3) Several authors have suggested that leadership stems from audacity and the verbal capacity to arouse fervent allegiance in others. Certainly these traits are indispensable if we are talking about the leadership of revolutionary change. Jesus, Mohammed, Churchill, Hitler, Mussolini, Roosevelt, and Kennedy were daring men who stirred deep devotion. They all had mastered the magic of speech for control.

In summary, the study of the traits of leaders shows the following:

1. The willingness and ability to work harder than most people.
2. The ability to analyze problems verbally—to "size up" situations.
3. The ability to speak clearly and to the point.
4. The ability to make suggestions in an attractive manner.
5. The ability to identify with the group to be led.

Yet the aspiring student leader must always remember that if heroes are made, not born, leaders are also chosen, not self-appointed. Leaders must be able to discern the norms of the aspirations and needs of the group.(4) Indeed, they must be able to verbalize those needs in vivid language so that the others of the group will find identification in the leader. Moreover, they must also be able to describe and to justify the action which will satisfy those needs. But when the leader speaks there is always the implied command: "This is what we must do!"

Leadership Roles

"All the world's a stage, and all the men and women merely players," said the bard. The person who takes center stage must know how to make many exits and entrances and to play many parts. Leadership roles fall into two main categories, variously called intellectual and emotional roles or instrumental and integrative roles. Very often the leadership in groups splits into these two roles, one or more persons furnishing the ideas and decisions and others helping the group to feel justified about its existence. Notice the sharp difference between the functions of the two following statements.

> "Every person must be present next Monday evening."
> "I think we have this project well on its way."

Whether the roles are played by the same or different people, it is important to know that in times of crisis it is the "integrative expressive" role which must be played well, or the leadership of the group is likely to change. For example we hear such things as: "OK, men that's enough. The job is done—good job! Take a day off." The emotional health of a group is maintained by other verbal acts (such as "Sure you can," "How about seeing Jim about this," "Sure, that isn't important to me," "I wanted you to know . . . ," "But this is the kind of effort we have to shoot for") and, most importantly, by restimulating the basic needs of the group. Integrative leadership is handled expertly, of course, only by those people who can read the hidden agenda with an eagle's eye and who are thus guided to make the appropriate commands.

The more intellectual kind of leadership deals with the logical processes, suggesting and seeking new ideas or information or opinions ("Yes, but I still think there is something more here . . ."), elaborating on suggestions, showing relationships, orienting the group to the goal when discussion flounders ("You are now saying . . . but, if I understand, isn't our main purpose. . . ?"), evaluating, energizing, and assisting with procedures—even to the more menial tasks of passing out papers, arranging the seating, and recording.

The top man in an organization, with several levels of command below, is obviously the directing force. He states the basic decisions. He tells what must be done.(5) Lower levels of authority are more likely to need skill in the integrative tasks. And while the capacity to shoulder responsibility and to make hard decisions is not so great at the in-between levels of leadership, those second and third in command must also be skillful users of speech skills. They must, on the one hand, be able to exercise some speech of control on their superiors (not at all an easy trick) and, in turn, they must be able to carry out the wishes of their superiors while they nurture the morale of their subordinates. As if that were not enough juggling, they must also be able to maintain effective communication in the unstable relationship with their competing equals.

Leadership and Human Contact

As one might suspect, the crucial leader in an organization is the one who can maintain verbal contact with the mass of men. And how does he best perform this task? The foreman, the teacher, the precinct worker who gets good results works closely with people and is perceived by his followers as pulling both for them and the organization, not for himself or for the organization alone. He appears to be most effective when he allows his men to "set their own pace." Gradually both governmental and business leaders are learning that it is not close, directing supervision that causes effective workers, but supervision that has intelligent concern for the emotional life of men.

The emotions of men in every kind of group enterprise are wisely accounted for when leaders recognize that all humans want to feel worthy and in the end are dependent for this on the comments of others, particularly from those with potential power over them.(6) The incomprehensible, violent, disorderly eruptions in schools, factories, and on the streets that cause us to shake our heads in despair stem from the prolonged frustrating failure of men to gain acceptance from those they respect. No greater leadership power exists than the expression of personal regard and a verbal pat on the back for an assignment well done. A professor is applauding with his usual academic restraint:

> I have been watching your development of this role for the past few weeks with particular interest. At first, and I was really worried, I thought you were going to bog down into a so-so performance. But you surely have developed a unique and powerful interpretation. Really first class!

Who is the student who does not grow a little even after such a sprinkle—particularly after a long drought?

A second and perhaps equally important issue is the clarity of leadership definition. The leader, through his control speech, defines not only his role and responsibilities but also those of his subordinates. Both children and men want to know what the limits are. It is extremely confusing not to know what is expected of you, to fail to understand what freedom of choice you have. How many times have you heard a parent talk to a child as follows:

> Come, Carol, show Auntie how you can dance. Up on your toes. . . . Now, now! Show-off! You like to tease, don't you? What a funny face. . . . But that's enough. That's enough, young lady. Carol, if you don't behave. . . . Now, Honey, don't cry. . . . Poor child. . . !

Ambiguity in our relationships with others is intolerable because it is in these relationships that we define ourselves. Sudden and careless changes in those relationships, particularly with authority figures, arouse anxiety and insecurity. The evidence also indicates that decentralized authority is more desirable and more productive, if the membership, in the main, really do want freedom.(7) In our society, most of us want to give some of the orders, and all of us want to know what we can do and what we cannot do.

The Format of a Command

We have said that those who wish to lead and to command must be able to express their directives clearly, attractively, and pointedly. This ability is not easily acquired. Officers in the military services must undergo thorough training before they are given responsibility. They are taught that brevity is important, that the longer the command, the more likely that it will be misunderstood or disobeyed. They learn that redundancy is usually essential: "Go to battle stations! Go to battle stations!" The words used should be simple, familiar words—the shorter, the better. Inflections must be imperative, with the implication being that the speaker expects that the order will be carried out—or else! The orders should be expressed fluently, not hesitantly. The voice should be strong, not weak in intensity. Some signal ("Attention!") should precede the command so that the men will be listening.

It is obvious that these requirements must be modified in civilian life where men have not been subjected to an intensive training program specifically designed to insure compliance. We soon learn that a softer approach is necessary, that signals such as a prefatory "Please" will bring cooperation much faster than a curt demand, that it is wise for the foreman to call the man by his first name before making the request, that saying, "I think we'd better empty that barrel" is more productive than "Empty that barrel!" We disguise the implied threat which underlies perhaps every real command by saying, "I'd appreciate it if you'd. . . ." Nevertheless, requests, directions, or orders must be phrased clearly, simply, and strongly if they are to be fulfilled.

As any student knows who has ever heard an instructor explaining a complicated assignment or procedure, it is always essential that the sequence or parts of the directive be stated as such. Terms such as *first, second, third,* and *then* will do much to eliminate confusion and insure performance. So will such phrases as "We've got to do *four* things if we're to get the job done. . . ." And almost always, there is the need for repetition. One-shot directions seldom find their target. The hypnotist finds in the repetition of his commands the very essence of his control. As Eisenson, Auer, and Irwin put it:

> Although we have said that listeners tend to believe and do as they are told, telling them only once may not be enough. Inattentiveness may mean that the listener fails to hear the stimulus words; simple inertia may keep him from taking them seriously; or he may receive them with skepticism or even hostility if they conflict with more potent habits of behavior, dominant attitudes, or strong beliefs. By employing the principle of summation of stimuli, however, succeeding repetitions of an idea normally encounter less resistance.*

The Content of Persuasive Speech

And what do we know about the content of speech designed to control? Perhaps the most significant overall generalization that we have been able to draw from the research is that *all argument is effective.* The trick is to get somebody to listen. "What holds attention determines action. . . . The impelling idea is simply the one which possesses the attention," said the psychologist William James. This generalization has been difficult to see in the mountain of data because most of the research bearing on the issue has been designed to see if an emotional argument is better than a logical one or if one

* From *The Psychology of Communication* (p. 283), by Jon Eisenson, J. Jeffrey Auer, and John V. Irwin. Copyright © 1963 by Meredith Publishing Company. Reprinted by permission of Appleton-Century-Crofts.

kind of organization is better than another, or if a speech in person is better than one on the radio. Some things seem to work better than others, but they all make their impact. Let us get the role of persuasive content in perspective. The data show that the human mind respects the information of the people it respects. Haiman, Paulson, and others have shown that the prestige of the speaker is an extraordinary force in change of attitude.(8) Berelson and Steiner, to whom we have referred earlier, conclude that men are persuaded and controlled more by the normative beliefs of the pople they talk to every day and the immediate groups to which they belong than by the so-called issues of the day.(9) Professional politicians do not rely basically on train stops and radio and television addresses. Political campaigns are won and lost largely by the grass roots workers in their conversations with their acquaintances. In Russia and China broadcasts on vital issues are made by radio to "opinion leaders," who in turn talk to the people for whom they are personally responsible. People are persuaded by people, not by information.

The answer to the question "What control speech is effective?" is not likely to be found in *what* is said, but in discerning the relative power of a variety of human relationships. Franklin H. Knower showed that logical and emotional appeals are equally effective, that men are more attracted to logical appeals than women are, that face-to-face appeals are more effective than audience situations, that men are more effective in audience situations than are women, and conversely that women are slightly more effective than men in face-to-face situations.(10) We all know that religious beliefs and human values are passed on through the family from generation to generation. Every great revolution in human thinking involves the breakdown of strong family ties, and every movement designed to conserve old human beliefs preaches the sanctity of the home. Belief is based on human relationships, not upon logical data.

People also are convinced by the kind of evidence they have been trained to respect, and this can be seen clearly in the following. During World War II in research done with soldiers, an effort was made to determine the wisdom of using the evidence on both sides of a controversial issue. The results indicated that those originally in favor of an argument were more highly influenced by the one-sided argument—of course, their own side.(11) Democrats at a convention are not interested in hearing the good word about Republicans. Listeners, however, who come to the meeting prejudiced against the argument are more likely to give the speaker a favorable response if he includes in his argument some of their pet data. And better educated people tend to like to hear both sides of the argument in a speech, more than less educated people do.

Further, at least one study shows that once a person has been persuaded by a speech incorporating evidence pro and con, he will be more stable, more resistant to a later speech on the opposite side, than will the listener who has heard just one side of the story.(12) It seems to add up to this: Being well informed on both sides of a controversial issue tends to stabilize one's attitude. This is probably the most comforting thought we can draw from the data.

One might like to conclude that educated people are persuaded from the weight of evidence. A careful examination, however, shows that the speaker using evidence on both sides always manages to demonstrate that the "evidence to the contrary" is ineffective, the argument of a "straw man." We shall illustrate the point by our own approach to the remainder of this discussion. Note the technique hidden in the following paragraph.

> Now there is little question that decisions are more likely to be wise if men examine the evidence on all sides before they draw conclusions. And we may hope, since men think as they are trained to think, that future education will train more people to be scientific, to respect conclusions based on the best available evidence. But to believe that the speaker who uses evidence on both sides in an argument is more fair or more rational or more likely to develop logical listeners than the speaker who presents only the evidence for his own side of the case is to fail to see the technique for what it is, simply a persuasive device. We have yet to see the persuader use the evidence to the contrary to show the wisdom of rejecting his own argument. People use evidence to the contrary in order to cite their prestige as knowledgeable people or to show that what on the surface appears to be a sound argument is not.

The Process of Speech for Control

There are two simple basic steps in the speech for control. First, the speaker explains what he wants the listeners to do or believe. "Let's go to the movies." "Did you know Mary is a terribly jealous person?" If the listener obliges or agrees, the speaker's urge to control has been satisfied by the first step. But if the listener ignores or resists, the speaker usually goes to work and doubles his effort to persuade. If we want to deceive ourselves as to what we usually do, we may say we "just present the evidence." But the evidence, if it is to be effective, is carefully selected to overwhelm the listener's objections. People who change their minds after strong resistance do so only after an experience of emotional excitement. If we are going to change the way people perceive and feel, we must stir them deeply.

There are two ways to do this—by appeal and by threat. The overall design of persuasion, then, may be seen in the following simple formula:

$$\text{Effectiveness of Persuasion} = \frac{\text{Appeal} + \text{Threat}}{\text{Inertia}}$$

Effective control speech must overcome inertia, the person's satisfaction with things as they are. The speaker stirs the famished desires and the latent fears of the listener. This is achieved by the magic of the identification process. As cited in the previous chapter, the listener begins to breathe in rhythm with the speaker. His heart begins to beat with that of the speaker. He tunes in. Physical conditions help or hinder this. People tend to fall into the rhythm of the speaker's voice and thought more readily when they are packed in close quarters than when they are scattered or alone—watching television, for instance. Father Coughlin, the famous radio priest of the Depression, found it necessary to get people to collect in homes around the radio in order to stir their passions.

The rhythm of primitive drums and dancing feet, the chanting of the church services, the shouting of the orator, the prolonged and exhausting argument over coffee cups, the music in the background all work to the same end. Excitation begins in rhythm. Any ROTC member can testify to the hypnotic effect of marching feet. And the more perfectly the squadron executes orders, the more spine-tingling the effect, for both participant and observer. "Marching kills thought. Marching makes an end of individuality."(13) Sargant, in *Battle for the Mind,* tells about the anthropologist who joined the native dance in order to understand their experience and fell into the hypnotic state of the dancers, and the uglier story of the young men who went to revival meetings because they found the girls susceptible to seduction following the meetings.(14) Even the "aha" experience of insight, the sudden understanding of something we have not known before, comes with, or just following, excitation. This is why, if we do not understand a proposition or theory we sometimes have to study until we become tired, upset, frustrated, and sometimes even angry before suddenly we comprehend. Excitation jostles the stuff in the head, and when it falls back into place, behold! the nonsense turns into sense. Those who would be creative drive themselves to the emotional experience that creates abreaction and new insight. Those who would control others must drive others until they suffer the change that leads to new perceptions.

You have doubtless read accounts where priests and political prisoners in police states have confessed to whatever crimes they were charged with. A recent "NBC White Paper" tells how innocent people, on the basis of their own confessions, have served prison terms. According to Sargant we all have our breaking point, at which we will confess anything our tormentor wants us to confess. People do not do this in order to escape terrible physical torture, which in fact is not really common in such inquisitions. One breaks down as rapidly as he becomes intensely emotional. So the tactics of professional inquisitors are designed to unstabilize. They drill the subject with questions until he is exhausted, then let him sleep for an hour, drill him two more hours, let him sleep all day. They awaken him in the middle of the night, threaten him, and give him a cigarette; console him and then put him in solitary confinement. The effect is to confuse him and to drive him to extreme loneliness. He is likely, in the end, to agree with his tormentor, because he so desperately needs somebody—anybody—with whom to identify. The little boy who has been shamed and spanked by his mother climbs upon her knee and huddles close because the one thing he cannot stand is rejection or isolation.

The essential act of persuasion is the stirring of the emotions of the listener. And as strange as it seems, emotional rebellion is just one step away from acceptance. One of the authors vividly recalls an extraordinarily malleable and fast-learning debater who, after each critique, exploded in profane and abusive rejection of the "stupid criticism." Then he changed his speech appropriately. The highly emotional atheist, communist, fascist, or democrat is just a step away from conversion to that which he denounces. It is the person who is not stirred who does not change. Excitation is basic and can be achieved by either appeal or threat.

The Appeal

The appeal or allure is most dramatically seen in the devices of the advertiser and the salesman. The object to be sold—the soap, beer, or cigarette—is associated with pleasing colors, pleasant sounds, alluring sex, or contemplation of heightened prestige and social position. Or for those of a more practical turn of mind, the appeal may be pitched for the desire to get something for nothing. Some of the economy models of small cars try to make themselves attractive on the basis of "what you do not get when you buy this automobile—power steering, for instance." But appeal, no matter what the twist may be, is designed to cause the receiver to be dissatisfied with the status quo, to be attracted to some other condition which is advantageous to the speaker. And the advertiser knows that the Promised Land must be seen within reach, tomorrow. Thus he stresses the low monthly payments or the availability—"Just pick up your phone." There is no man so dissatisfied as the one who almost has what he wants. Hope means almost.

In the main, the advertiser and the salesman are content with appeal, though not always. For instance, deodorant advertisements visualize the success of the sweet-smelling person but also show the social failure of those who are offensive. Insurance companies like to remind the listener of the possibilities of the death of the breadwinner. If, in haberdashery advertisements, success is predicted for the man who dresses the part, the suggestion is left that inappropriate dress accompanies failure. So advertisers do use threat, if gently, though pleasant appeal is more predominant.

The reasons are not obscure. The advertiser is selling comfort. Better homes, automobiles, foods, and the gadgets of the industrial age have come into being out of an underlying love for luxury and comfort. In the end the advertiser would probably undermine his own world if he excited too many painful feelings.

There is another factor involved. In the main, in a competitive market, the only thing the seller has to offer us is preference. If we do not buy Palmolive, there is Sweetheart, Cameo, Dial, or Ivory. Threat pressure is of little use on human beings where personal preference is involved. Only appeal works. For instance, in one study fifty executives were put under group pressures in an effort to see how well they would stand by their beliefs and perceptions.(15) Few of them could independently decide as to whether, for instance, one of two lines was longer than the other. If they believed the majority of their colleagues were seeing the reverse of what their eyes told them, they tended to discredit their eyes. They seemed, on the other hand, almost completely unswayed by group preference, say for a given color or sound. Apparently people tend to feel that their tastes are personal and good.

We have said earlier that one of the traits of leadership is the ability to size up a situation and to respond appropriately. This means that anyone who desires to command others must be able to recognize the needs of those he desires to control. To appeal means to understand the needs of others. All the great leaders throughout history have had this ability, but it is just as essential for the least of us, even if our aspiration is only to persuade our wives to cook a good evening meal. Our own personal needs for domination or management are not enough. Even the controlling child must be able to assess the degree to which he can boss his parents around. We must be able to empathize with those we would control well enough so they will not reject our requests or demands. Often it is necessary for those who wish to lead to be able to verbalize the needs of others even better than the others can do themselves. We must share the lives of those we would control if we wish them to accept our suggestions gratefully. This means that we must always phrase our demands in appropriate language. The robber can yell "Hands up!" if he has a pistol, but no clerk can as peremptorily command his boss to raise his salary. We must phrase our urges to control as supplications, requests, suggestions, or demands only after surveying our relationships with those we seek to manage.

> Those who make demands must be able, of course, to estimate the probability of compliance. Often it is possible to create a climate of compliance by programming our requests so that our listeners get into the patterns of responding positively.(16) Ever since Eve, wives have managed to conquer their husbands by such a method. They tell them to do the things they had already planned to do. They get their ultimate control through a cumulative programming of graduated demands that is as fiendishly scientific as it is instinctive. We still find it hard to believe that Machievelli was a man.

The Threat

Threat is a warning of impending punishment and injury. Its use is as old as the cave. An old text on education rescued from the sands of Egypt says, "A boy's ears are on his back. He listens when he is beaten." The threat persists today. All the studies show that we are extremely sensitive to social pressures as well as to stripes on the back, and one of the most powerful threats the persuader can use is a description that suggests our relationships with other people hang in the balance. How often we hear something like: "I'm telling you, if the Old Man finds out there's going to be plenty of trouble!"

Some researchers find that attitudes toward social issues are the easiest ones to alter.(17) Perhaps social threat is so impelling because social fact is so scarce. How can one prove the destructive results of federal aid to education or that prosperity has been caused by the good judgment of the President? The similarity of the cases compared and contrasted are outside the scientific world of testing. It naturally follows that if one does not really have any facts the only arguments left are the prestigious names of famous people who agree with the speaker and the historical analogies which make first class drama, second class logic, and third class science. In addition, where the facts are few and questionable, ambiguity is high. As we learned from a previous chapter ambiguity arouses fear. So the persuader capitalizes on this and shouts the dangers. Indeed, the very absence of facts makes persuading all the easier. You have doubtless heard the story about the minister who wrote in the margins of his sermon manuscript, "Evidence very thin here—shout like hell." Shouting excites, and excitation is easiest where the facts are scarce.

The Design of the Threat

In all persuasive effort, aside from advertising and salesmanship, the threat is a key feature. (People want new clothes because clothes wear out—so the appeal of new clothes may be enough.) But beliefs do not wear out so readily as shoes and, indeed, our most cherished ones have a way of improving in looks and durability the longer we wear them. Thus, it is difficult to appeal to a man to believe differently. A plethora of studies shows that the only belief to which it is easy to appeal is the one a man already has. And this attempt to reinforce the beliefs that already exist is what is done in the main at churches and political halls. To ask a man to *believe* differently is to ask him to exchange the foundations of his life, and foundations of buildings or lives are not easily replaced. "It is wonderful to think as I think" will not alone arouse the excitation that shifts belief unless the listener is already thoroughly frustrated by his present belief. Appeal to radically new beliefs, attitudes, and feelings must be supplanted or at least supplemented, by some kind of terror. Although very few people seem to believe in the Inferno described by Dante, almost all people believe in the existence of many devils. In short, to frighten the listener so that he gets the crawling feeling that he is stalked by a dangerous devil is the most effective device the persuader has to induce the listener to conjure that enemy. "What a task confronts the American clergy," complained a minister, "preaching good news of a Savior to people who for the most part have no real sense of sin." (18)

It is interesting to recognize that all threats are couched in one of three ways. There is the threat that you had better obey or you'll get hurt by some mysterious power, the threat that you had better conform or you'll hurt yourself, and the third threat: "Do what I say or I'll clobber you myself." Let us examine each in more detail.

1. "They" will hurt you. The Communists will attack. The Chinese will take over. The kids will get out of hand. Either you "do like I say" or else somebody, "your enemy," will hurt you.

The enemy camps in the background of every effective debate case. Irrespective of topic, the essentials are always these:

Affirmative	*Negative*
1. Need for change. (Conditions are bad. If we do not make changes the enemy will take over.)	1. There is no need for a change. (The so-called enemy is a paper tiger. Things are not perfect, but correction is taking place within the present framework.)
2. Plan. (This plan will eliminate the enemy, in the following way.)	2. Or, conditions are bad, but in a way different than the affirmative states. (There is an enemy, but not the one the affirmative describes.)
	3. The plan of the affirmative creates problems they have not recognized. (Let me describe the hidden enemy the affirmative does not see.)

2. "You are going to hurt yourself." You are your own enemy. This is the favorite of parents and teachers. If you do not change your ways you will get into trouble. "Think, feel, and do as I say or you will fall into deep trouble."

The threat "You are bad, you are your own enemy and will fall by your own hands," no matter how well-intentioned, results in tragedy of the greatest consequence. A boy so taught by his father may learn to resist believing almost anything his father says, but one thing he cannot resist—conceiving himself in the way his father describes him. "You're lazy." "You never do anything right." Everywhere you go there's trouble." These things may be said verbally or nonverbally. Either way, the boy always hears what his father says about him. The hated teacher may teach very little, but one thing he teaches for sure—the attitudes he feels toward the student. One's peers have this power too. When he hears them jeer, "Hi, Powder Puff!" a small boy's muscles tend to melt. Those who assess the college scene say that 75 per cent of the change in a college student in the course of four years (good and bad) must be ascribed to the student's social environment, not to his courses. These changes are the work of speech, yes, but of speech infused with social threat.

The devastating race hatred in Africa, according to one source, results from the white man's success in persuading the natives to hate their own traditions and yet not love European traditions.(19) Apparently the excitation aroused by hearing derogatory statements about ourselves, regardless of the way we perceive the speaker, *makes us vulnerable to his view of us*. Thus we learn to hate ourselves, as well as him. Thus we come to lose our citizenship in life, to become strangers on these shores, alienated from ourselves and others. This is the tragic result of threatening speech which conjures the enemy in the listener himself.

3. "I will hurt you. I am your enemy. Either you do as I say or else." This is the way of the pathological persuader. The threat of the speaker is the most likely one to alter behavior and the least likely to persuade favorable beliefs and feelings. The rapist offers his victim her life for compliance. Thus he controls behavior. He is somewhat less successful in convincing her to consider some of his more interesting philosophical views on life. The speaker who desires to change beliefs and attitudes usually does not allow himself to be conceived as the enemy.

Listen to the speech of people in charge:

"All right, either we get this done today, or everybody. . . ."
"This is compromise of basic principles and invites ultimate destruction."
"Friday afternoon is the deadline." (That's a fascinating word—the *deadline*.)
"Read the next chapter and be ready for a test."
"If you'll make a three point this winter, I'll get you a new set of clubs in the spring."
"I wouldn't shout if you would stop nagging me."
"You could make something of yourself if you tried."
"I love you, but. . . ."

Threat saturates much of our speech. Few of us fail to hear the bad grammar in "Don't never do that no more." Many of us cannot assess the impact of the statement.

We are quite aware we have dramatized the threat so frequent in control speech, but we do not feel we have exaggerated. It seems to us that threat is one of the chief ingredients of the social air we breathe and that we grow up dulled to the impact of threatening speech. Thus, we are all the more vulnerable and all the more dangerous to others, in the end. The stick is becoming less common in most social circles, but the threatening tongue, often subtle, pervades our homes and schools. Even youngsters in the elementary school learn to fear that their grades will not open the door to their future. Arriving at college, our students, the cream of the intellectual crop, suffer serious doubts about their intellectual powers. Need we say more? Fear of the person in charge pervades the social order. We wish it were not so, but we are not afraid to look at it squarely.

If one doubts the significance of threat in control speech, let him try to erase all threat from his own speech in his leadership roles. We have spent many years at the task and we know that every time we refuse to challenge another, when we want our way, we confront ourselves with the challenge of discovering the genuine traits of leadership within ourselves.

A Case Study in the Speech for Control

All this is dramatically demonstrated by the persuasive techniques used by the Chinese captors of American soldiers in the Korean War. Their success was attested by the apathy of the 4,000 prisoners returned to American custody after the war, and even more so, by the number of confessions and traitorous statements previously signed by American boys, published by the Chinese, and distributed throughout the world. At first these were thought to be confessions rung from men on the rack, but later it was learned that the Chinese did not use the diabolical techniques of detective thrillers, but the simple techniques of speech designed for control. Let us see the formula at work.

1. First, the boys were herded into a compound and given a speech by a *young* communist who spoke *G.I. English* which he had perfected in an American university. He said something like this: "Welcome to the People's State. You, of course, do not want to be here. But here you are. We shall feed and take care of you as best we can, not so well as you are accustomed, but as best we can. Nobody is going to get hurt here like American propaganda would have you believe. When we get organized we shall provide you education, in order to help you put in your time. And when the

war is over we shall send you back to your good homes and we hope you stay there." (The substance of the message was the *we-are-your-friends* appeal.)

2. Then the boys were turned loose for six months in the compound without sufficient food, clothing, and shelter. Life was highly disorganized and the necessaries were extremely limited. Of 7,000 prisoners, 3,000 died in this six months. Physical conditions were bad, but not such as to account for the high mortality. A little imagination suggests that frustration and emotional upheaval were intense. Most Americans had had little training for survival in near starvation conditions and total social disorganization. It requires skill to live "on the edge of nothingness," and apparently the pressures of the environment were so radically different from that which they had been trained to live in that many died. The rest were conditioned for the next stage. (The intent was obviously to unstabilize the men.)

3. The men were herded into outdoor lecture halls in which they listened, while standing, to lectures lasting four and five hours. A tedious story of every social injustice in the American climb to wealth was recounted while the principles and ideals of communism were extolled. In the afternoon the boys were gathered into groups of twelve where they were orderd to tell what they had heard in the morning. They did not have to agree, just explain what they had heard. If one of the group did not talk, none of the group were permitted to eat that night. One can imagine the pressure on the deviant in the group. Thus, by enforced listening and talking the American soldier gradually came to understand and accept communism, at least as something one may contemplate without horror. (The reward appeal of food and the threat of no food worked hand in hand to produce the desired behavior.)

4. The Chinese provided opportunities for the boys to play ball, put on plays, write camp newspaper articles, paint pictures. However, in order to participate in these extramural activities one had to demonstrate cooperative and friendly behavior toward his captors. And if one acted in a play, the drama had to be acceptable to communistic ideology. The boys saw no harm. They, of course, did not know their articles and paintings were being duplicated by the thousands and sent to all parts of the world. (The Chinese appealed to the soldier's self-interest, by the reward of an immediate advantage.)

5. The Chinese figured out an ingenious way to break down the cohesion (loyalty) among the boys too. They rewarded a boy with candy, cigarettes, and money if he would tell about any antisocial behavior he observed in the group. In any group, particularly where frustration is high, fighting, stealing food, misappropriating each other's few belongings will occur. The boy who would report an incident would be rewarded. Informing is considered one of the lowest forms of behavior in our culture. When the victim is pun-

ished, the group usually turns against the informer. But the Chinese did not punish the one informed on. They were interested not in finding culprits but in making them, and the boys did not see this. Why not inform then? The informer received his reward and nobody was hurt. One report states that two out of every five boys became an informer. Soon no one could trust anybody else. (By a system of appeal to self-interest the Chinese broke down community among the boys.)

6. By the very same techniques—informing—the Chinese taught the boys to conceive of themselves as their own personal enemies. The captors, again, gave small favors to the boys if they would stand up in a group and tell about their own shortcomings, inform on themselves. This is a police state tactic as old as the first inquisition, and a child-rearing device as old as the first authoritarian parent. "Johnnie, stand up and say you are sorry!" The Korean War prisoner was taught, in like fashion, to undermine himself. The crucial techniques in speech for control are those that cause the victim to lose faith in himself. (At the command of a basic appeal, men often exchange their birthright for a bowl of pottage.)

7. The last device was simply an intensification of the communication designed to alienate the soldier from his "tribal allegiances." Only "Dear John" letters and notices from collection agencies and complaints by wives and sweethearts about the terrible TV programs were delivered to the men. Letters of love and hope and yearning did not reach their destination. Thus, the men received a distorted view of the attitudes and feelings of the most important people in their lives, those people upon whom they leaned for emotional support.

Reflection upon this cursory explanation of one plan for speech control indicates vividly the roles of excitement by both appeal and threat. Emotional instability is created most effectively by destroying confidence in the basic relationships of a person with himself and others. All persuasive efforts (except in salesmanship) may be analyzed within this framework. The differences, from case to case, are in the degree of appeal and threat. You will note, from your own experience, the more the persuader has decided he must control, the more the threat and the greater its intensity.

A Critique of Speech for Control

One cannot examine the social order without recognizing the necessity for the speech of control. A society of all chiefs and no Indians will not work. And old social abuses to which time accustoms us, such as the parental mistreatment of children, the plight of the aged and the poverty-stricken in a land of plenty, are not corrected until somebody stands up and cries out with a voice that stirs the emotions of men. Stagnation and social corruption seem to fall in on all societies, in all ages, like walls of sand. Awakening and renovation and maintenance of some semblance of the human dream is a part of the work of every generation. We need control speech.

Yet one cannot look long at the speech for control as practiced before he discovers its abuses. A clarion call seldom arouses only men of good conscience. Even the perceptive Jesus selected his own Judas. The man of words usually helps others see the evil in a vicious system. But when the revolution is done and the new order is established, it usually incorporates most of the old evils—as one hundred years of Negro freedom illustrate.

It is our belief, however, that man is not destined to be the victim of this cycle, that we can eventually solve the problem of the abuses of control speech, even as now we can escape the gravity of the earth. But if we do, we must ferret out the practice that creates the evil cycle. It seems to us that we humans accord too much dignity to our feelings of hatred and thereby get trapped into the misuse of the magical power of speech to control others. Hatred is a convenient instrument for mobilizing the energies of a person or a group for defense, but hatred is a Trojan horse. We take it in, and it turns on us and kills the values we wanted to defend. To attack is to emulate that which we hate. No man rises above his behavior.

We are saying this: Speech for control is necessary in our society and is therefore not to be deplored. But we have yet to learn that the speech of threat is too often the speech of hate, and that the speech of hate is a boobytrap. Here is a fictitious piece of "Capitol Talk," the real counterpart of which you may read almost any week in the newspaper.

> I will not be baited into a verbal struggle with the Senator. Communist leaders all over the world would be happy to see a bitter name-calling contest between the Senator and me at this crucial hour. I will make no further comment, but I confess I am greatly distressed that the Senator has unfortunately seen fit to play the political game even when American lives are at stake. . . .

The speech of threat may be as blunt as "I dare you to refuse" or as indirect as the above. In either case we have the speech for control out of control. Somehow we must learn to create the desire for change by appeal alone.

6 Speech for Thought and Thought for Speech

Even though we spend much of our lives with other people, most of our conversation is silent—in self-communion, in thought. Truly, much that we call thoughts are but wisps of vague awarenesses floating through "the palace of shadows" known as the brain. All of us often have a feeling that there are things that should be said which we cannot say. Thinking is often laborious, incomplete, even painful. Through thinking we have conquered the earth, but we fear we think poorly most of the time. The speaker who would say something of value must think of the problems of thought.

If it were not that this silent world of thought is so utterly important we would ignore the topic, for the truth is that we do not know much about thought and its interrelationships with speech. It is not that we lack relevant information, but rather, that we cannot be sure of its meanings. The nerves have been traced into the brain mass. Localization of function, interrelating areas, cellular structure, and brain waves have all been studied in great detail. An unceasing stream of research reports flow from the laboratories. But the famous neurophysiologist, R. W. Gerard, has said that the implications of this knowledge for an understanding of the way we think and learn to think is not much greater than if "for all we knew the cranium were stuffed with cotton wadding."(1) What we say in this chapter, then, is a selection of nonbiological information which we feel has implications for students of speech. We present this explanation in the hope that the student may contemplate his experience as a thinking creature, and be attracted to more thinking behavior, for it seems to us that the thinking of the world, except in scientific exploration, is chaotic indeed.

Most of us experience the feeling that our thinking *is* silent speech. When we are deep in a difficult problem we often catch ourselves saying aloud, "Hm, could be, uh, let's see. . . . No, . . . How about this. . . ?" John B. Watson and other behavioristic psychologists believed that speech and thought were one, and they demonstrated that incipient movements of the muscles about the mouth and throat take place when the person thinks. Then a doubting Thomas anesthetized the mouth of a subject, who continued to think, thus discouraging investigation of the relationship for years. That some relationship exists is inescapable. Both Sapir and Whorf argue that a man's thinking is confined within and affected by the peculiar structure of the language he speaks.(2) Considerable differences have been cited among the thought processes of Germans, Chinese, and Indians. But, as Harvard professor Joshua Whatmough points out, Germans, Chinese, Indians, and all other peoples seem to respond in a host of similar ways too.(3) Nevertheless, no one today disputes the close relationship between language and thought. Most psychologists, however, are more likely to conclude that while we think with speech and language, we can also think without silent speech.(4) Or if you like, we seem to think in many different "languages." Mathematics, architecture, music, painting, sculpturing, photography, and dancing are language systems, too, by which we express ourselves symbolically. Thinking need not be done in the mother tongue. Yet the language of speech has a kind of special place in human thought. We shall look at the peculiar advantages of spoken language as we proceed. For the moment we should like to make the point again: speech and thought are not identical, but speech is an important tool of thought.

WHAT IS THINKING?

The human makes tools, and among the most important of these tools are symbols which he can substitute for objects and actions. Moreover, he can manipulate these symbols. When he does so, he is thinking. A symbol is something that stands for something else. The characters on this page, for instance, stand for the words of human speech. The words men speak, "moon," "strike," "golden," stand for things, actions, and qualities. At another level of abstraction, white can stand for purity, a rock for stability, the heart for human affection. And so it is in science too. A foot stands for a unit of distance and a cubic centimeter of water stands for a gram. The essence of thought then is the metaphor, one thing standing for another. The world is many things related and even changing into each other under certain conditions. So love may turn into hate, food into energy, ice into water, vegetation into coal—and vice versa. The symbol is man's creation, his invention to reflect and express his awareness of the relationships and magical changes of one thing into another. Thinking is making and manipulating analogies, comparing similar but unique things, and creating new combinations of symbols when in our mental tumbling we stumble onto new relationships for which we have no name.

The power to symbolize is so much a part of us we fail to see it as the essence of our humanity. The story of Helen Keller's discovery that things have names, and the impact of this knowledge on her mental processes is thrillingly illuminating. Helen Keller was made blind and deaf by disease at the age of nineteen months. For the next five years she grew without normal word contact. At seven, when Miss Sullivan came as her teacher, Helen was a headstrong, undisciplined, and unruly little animal.

Within a day or two Miss Sullivan had taught Helen a few words, by spelling them into her hand. But Helen did not at first grasp the implications of the code: *Everything has a name.* In her still unlighted mind Helen confused the word signs for "mug" and "water." One morning, about a month after Miss Sullivan's arrival, she and Helen went to the pump in the garden. What happened is vividly told by Miss Sullivan.

> I made Helen hold her mug under the spout while I pumped. As the cold water gushed forth, filling the mug, I spelled "w-a-t-e-r" into Helen's free hand. The word coming so close upon the sensation of cold water rushing over her hand seemed to startle her. She dropped the mug and stood as one transfixed. A new light came into her face. She spelled "water" several times. Then she dropped on the ground and asked for its name and pointed to the pump and the trellis, and suddenly turning around she asked for my name. . . . In a few hours she had added thirty new words to her vocabulary.(5)

Helen had grasped the key that opens the human universe. Let us see this experience in the words of Helen Keller as she explained it years later.

> We walked down the path to the well-house, attracted by the fragrance of the honeysuckle with which it was covered. Someone was drawing water and my teacher placed my hand under the spout. As the cool stream gushed over one hand she spelled into the other the word water, first slowly, then rapidly. I stood still, my whole attention fixed upon the motion of her fingers. Suddenly I felt a misty consciousness as of something forgotten—a thrill of returning thought; and somehow the mystery of language was revealed to me. I knew then that "w-a-t-e-r" meant the wonderful cool something that was flowing over my hand. That living word awakened my soul, gave it light, hope, joy, set it free! (6)

Miss Keller goes on to say, "As we returned to the house every object which I touched seemed to quiver with life." "In the beginning was the word," says the Ancient Book. Without words humans live on the plane of the beast. Human thought is not words, nor need be expressed in words, but very often it seems to come into existence through them.

Direction of Thought

The German psychologist, Ach, long ago focused attention upon the magic of the *aufgabe*, the "determining tendency." In all thinking there seems to be in the beginning only a kind of restless urge to create a symbol pattern. Recent authors have called it *cognitive dissonance*. A vague irritation overcomes inertia, and then, once we start, each act seems to cue off the next. For example, the first few words of this sentence determine the way the *sentence* —— ——. You were almost certain to say "the sentence will end" or words of similar meaning. To become a freshman is to set one's course for becoming a sophomore. The value of a business venture exceeds the value of all the buildings and equipment, accounting for an intangible known as the "worth of the going concern." In physics we call it momentum. The "directioning tendency" is the momentum of thought.

Over and over again, when we have asked students why they enrolled in our course in speech they have answered, "I want to learn to be able to think on my feet." What they mean is that they wish to be able to start with a dim, embryonic hunch of a thought and to help it emerge, one appropriate word following another until, lo! the formulation is complete and adequate. They want to be able to think aloud and with ease. They know of course that none of us, except in special circumstances, ever rehearses word for word a thought which is to be expressed. We begin with a felt need to say something. We dimly know what we want to say, but the actual verbal programming takes place only after we start moving our mouths.

Sometimes it comes out wrong. Our formulation somehow failed to match the vague internal model we had in mind. We are not sure just what that model was, but we do know we said something other than what we had intended. When this happens we take another stab at it, saying it differently. When our utterance does match, we know it immediately and feel good about it. We admire those speakers who seem to be able to choose the appropriate words, one after another, so that each contributes to the development of the thought that finally completes itself. To be able to start with only the determining tendency, the hunch, and to fluently turn this into clearly verbalized thought seems almost magical, and we want to be able to master that magic.

Can this be taught? We are not sure. Can it be learned? Of this we are certain, because we have seen many an incoherent, faltering student turn into an excellent speaker, one who could think on his feet, one who could speak his thoughts fluently and well. How did he learn this skill? We are not sure, but we know that he had to have many experiences in verbal formulation of thought before he did master it. The way is the speech way. You can't learn to think on your feet if you rest silently on your bottom.

We know that these students who learned to think aloud with fluency and precision did some mental pot-boiling before they did open their mouths, that they stirred the stillborn thought, half verbalizing to themselves silently and in a sort of free associative sort of fashion, sketching the outlines of the pattern that could only get completed by the utterance itself. Though the thoughts they spoke were not rehearsed at all in the actual words that would code them later, deep in the semiconscious recesses of the mind the pattern was forming. This is how books and artistic compositions are born, and probably even the most ordinary thought too. Thoughts have their origins in the *aufgabe*, in the directional intent.

The directional intent is a part of all our speech. Here is one example of it in dormitory talk.

> Hey, Bud, ever get the hunch you were meant for better things? All fooling aside, I was wondering this morning what a guy ought to do after he gets out of this educational ratrace. I think I'd like to travel. . . . I'm no bum but I mean I get the feeling I don't know what it's all about and if I could see some of the world, different people, maybe I'd know where I ought to put my dime. Sometimes I get the feeling nobody around here really knows what he is doing. . . . They're just in a helluva big hurry to do it. . . .

This conversation, once set off, ran long into the night.

The hunch, emerging from feelings—often beyond the reach of words—is the beginning of all thinking, and it takes on deeper significance as we comprehend the early growth of a person. Piaget, the Swiss psychologist, studied children to see how the human gradually comes to speak and to think. He observed that we spend our first years learning how to see, touch, and hear the world of space and sound. All this we do before our memories begin to store symbol patterns, and so we have the illusion that we have always known how to see and hear. But those who gain sight for the first time in adult life, see at first only a fireworks of flashing light, and they have to close their eyes and feel the apple, before they can look at it and make sense of the light messages. The child's first challenge in a world full of static and changing light is to acquire some sense of physical reality. He learns in just a few weeks to tune in on the human voice, and this is the root of speech. He learns to fondle things, to hang on, and from this he gathers information. At six months he reaches up to be held. He learns how to "track" a moving object, especially his mother's face. In the nonverbal speech of physical contact, again with his mother in particular, he learns his basic feelings about himself and others. Gradually, as he acquires words for things, he begins to talk to things as well as to people. Listen to a child talking to his toys. "Go here. That's good. Up zoooooum." Sometimes it is incomprehensible to the adult.

Perhaps the first foundations of meaning lie in the emotions. We learn to react affectively to people and things long before we learn to identify them, certainly in language. "Meanings precede objects in perception," says Joseph Church.(7) Our whole thinking life rides on an ocean of feeling. The basic role of emotion in thinking may be observed if we notice the way a person calls up an old memory. We asked a friend, "You went to Jamaica one winter, didn't you?" "Yes," he said, "Jamaica is a beautiful country; the water is so clear, the forests are unspoiled, and the people wear the cleanest clothes. . . ." First he spoke of his feelings and then he documented them.(8)

Every proposition begins "I am for," "I am opposed," or "I don't give a ——." Robert Teller, the father of the H-bomb, argued in the years preceding the bomb testing ban that present and future life is little endangered by the strontium 90 in the atmosphere. The Nobel Prize winning chemist, Linus Pauling, argued with the same evidence that we doom thousands of the unborn. The facts involved concern the relative threats of communism and bomb testing. The available facts are not unquestionably clear and they do not lend themselves to any scientific comparison. Underneath the argument are the feelings, on the one hand, "I am *concerned* for saving our skins," on the other, "I am *more concerned* for protecting the unborn."

We do not thus take a poke at a couple of scientists or discredit the human race for its emotional orientation or conclude that a more sophisticated man would rise above his emotions. What we are emphasizing in comparing the thought and speech of Teller and Pauling is that their logical processes are directed down conflicting paths because their affections are attached to different values.

But above all, for his potential growth, the child learns in the first two years how to be comfortable or uncomfortable in his social environment—how to tend toward, away from, or against people. And if you note the speech of those around you, you will hear the phrases that reflect postures learned early in life. The spirit of a person is woven into his speech. Only recently have we become sensitive to the crucial significance of the emotional imprinting of the first two years. (9) During the blitz in London, new-born babies in the hospitals were fed, bathed, and changed, but received the minimum fondling and comforting sounds of a mother's voice. Reports by the psychiatrist Bowlby, and others, state that these children, now in early adulthood, learn poorly and make poor adjustment to people of all ages of both sexes. A subsequent United Nations report about the role of a mother, or mother substitute, in the first months of life states that a child who lacks the loving voice and touch of a loving adult for six months fails to develop emotionally. (10) If the lack persists for two years the child fails to attach his life to others. They cannot love or even really hate other people, so they have little reason to talk except for the fulfillment of their immediate physical needs. They are ineffective. They do not plan. They cannot think except in the most elementary way. Abstract reasoning and talk are beyond them.

There is a tendency deep in the human to be attracted to think, to be attracted to talk about complex problems.(11) Conversely, to discharge all tension and to make the usual cargo of one's speech as light as, "Where are you going this summer?" or "Should have seen the baseball game on television last night," is to demonstrate the behavior of a defective or diseased organism. Harlow, the learning theorist, says the urge to solve a puzzle is as great as the drive to have all problems solved—in the healthy human.(12) Normal humans are attracted to that which is initially incongruous. Even the rat crosses the electrically charged cage to examine the other side.(13) "Why does the chicken cross the road?" asks the comedian. "To get to the other side," shouts his partner, who probably does not know he is making a profound remark. Many humans, and unfortunately they do not know it, turn chicken and will not cross the road, for they are all tangled in approach-avoidance conflicts. It is extremely important for us humans to be programmed with appropriate emotions very early in life if we are going to be attracted to think and to talk about our complex and confusing world. You may have noticed that the thinking person often talks like this:

> I think what I am trying to say is. . . . No, that isn't it . . . somehow somewhere in this stuff there's a point. . . . How come, this ought to be easy. . . . Maybe we ought to look at it this way. . . .

To feel at home with a quest and a question is the emotional need of the person who thinks. The attraction to a problem—the love to explore—is the first step in speech that involves thinking.

The Role of the Unconscious

Let us here examine the real magic beneath our verbal processes. Taking a deep dive down into the sea of our existence, we may discover comprehensions and techniques that release our speech and give it power. All of us have the illusion that what we do is always consciously selected—an illusion perhaps created by speech itself, which is so available for examination. Yet, without any firm belief or disbelief about the design of the unconscious, we all recognize that we really do not even know what we are going to say until we hear ourselves saying it. Fifty students, for instance, speak on the same topic, but each speaks a unique combination of words, and if by some strange chance one should speak the same words as his neighbor he will be charged at least with breaking the law of averages. The professor's doubts about the innocence of one or both students testifies to his observation that language wells up out of the unconscious—or if not, he is led to the stranger conclusion, that the brain is a scrambling machine.

Man has probably always felt that his life is partially hidden to himself. Sigmund Freud lifted out the unconscious—the area of the unknowable—to explain much of the unexplainable about our thought and speech. A man says "I detest administration," but he refuses to give up administrative tasks. A girl says, "I'm through with that guy," and then she marries him. Speech does not have access to all our mental life. How important it is for us to understand the voice of the unconscious we do not know. But we do know that thought, like the captain of a ship, is on call night and day. If a person is awakened each time he begins to dream, as may be recognized in an electroencephalograph of brain waves, within a few days he grows weary, irritable, and uneven in emotional stability. (14) Sleep and night dreams permit the ship of our verbal, conscious world to sail on with even keel.

Much of our conscious decision-making is done on the basis of messages that are no more explainable than inclinations or hunches. The verbal, conscious world is what separates us from the beasts, to be sure, but it is a misguided man indeed who feels that he chose his mate (who will govern much of his future life) or selected his profession (which will govern his life almost as much as his mate) or picked his friends (who will help him tolerate both his mate and work) with a conscious examination of the facts. The future heralds itself but it never presents itself until it becomes the present. Most of our important decisions have to be made on hunches.

And, once again, what does this have to do with speech? Any student who really allows his thought processes to design a speech for him finds the logical order for it not before he prepares, but as he prepares. He talks out or writes out his speech and in this preparing process he discovers what he knows comes from his unconscious nowhere, especially if he respects that nowhere as he should. Inspiration, we call it. The craft of putting things together in their most artistic, and therefore most effective, form comes as we proceed. To insist upon formula from the beginning of any task is to cut ourselves off from the unconscious. We are all schizophrenic in the sense that our thinking is done in part by the symbolic elves who inhabit the skull. And if we but listen, they often whisper revelations of wisdom which the verbal world may express but cannot discover.(15) Only those deeply aware of that mysterious unconscious self, make the most effective partnership with the unconscious self.

> What we are saying is that each of us should occasionally explore as much of this area of the unconscious as is permitted to us. We should be willing to let our thoughts run where they will, to throw away the conscious controls and see what comes out of the unconscious. Day dreaming and night dreaming show that this is possible. We would feel it worthwhile for any student to read James Joyce's *Ulysses* and then to compose verbal snatches of his own similar book. Our minds are stored with riches of which we are but dimly aware. In its deeps are stored a thousand sunken galleons that once sailed our conscious seas. Perhaps there are monsters down there in the depths but there is also treasure. All thought, like all living things, originally comes from the sea.

The Association of Symbols

As we get acquainted with any new topic or idea, we tumble the words around in order to get the feel of relationship. In so doing we invariably come upon new words which we handle much as we did a tennis racket the first time we grasped it. We half sound-out the new word, feel its weight, and strike it against another word. A word alone has little more meaning than a lonely girl on a desert isle—except to the first sailor. Meaning comes as a word finds its companion. Thus the manipulation of thought is the scrambling of words in a multitude of combinations until we come upon that phrase that satisfies our purpose. Note the peculiar savor of the following:

The New Frontier
Always the Young Strangers
Gone with the Wind
The Iron Curtain
To the victor go the spoils.

Phrases catch on because the peculiar combination of words captures a thought.

Dewey noted that the second step in thinking is that of defining or capturing the problem, and this is very close to what we are talking about. Piaget observed that this exploration of association is the second stage in thinking that the child goes through from the age of two to seven. He is learning while verbalizing what goes with what in the physical world. He learns that a balloon and watermelon are the same size, but different in weight, and the same or different in color and quite dissimilar in taste. Thus he abstracts characteristics and sees things as combinations of characteristics. This symbolic manipulation leads to the power to represent, so that even a five-year-old is able to understand the symbolic equivalence when he sees the earth among planets on a television screen, or a horse in a book, or himself in the looking glass. He now no longer tries to pick up shadows and streaks of light. He learns that beads separated over the length of the string do not make more beads than they do when they are pushed together. Pushing them together he throws up his hands and says, "See!" Upon several trials he stops being Simple Simon and learns the futility of trying to carry water in a sieve. He looks in the sieve and verbalizes his lesson: "Aw' gone." After trying to jump and stay up in the air, he ceases abruptly and stares vacantly. Silently or aloud he codifies his experience in words, and this is how he tucks away the knowledge that he will need another day. And now he no longer looks into the hands to find the noise of the clap. He pushes over a stack of blocks and thus learns what *causes* the tumbling. "Two blocks are higher than one," he says to himself. He discovers with surprise that one can have *two* blocks as well as *two* ears. If one puts the lid on the box, the toys do not go away by magic. Take off the lid and there they are! If you put the ball in the washing machine, you can take the ball out. There is process and reverse process. But he still may make some amusing causal errors! The swaying trees make the wind blow and the thunder makes it rain.

Having reached adulthood, it is difficult for us to remember how much we learned by manipulating things, and talking all the while. But to sense the significance of that early symbolic play is to recognize, perhaps sadly, how much more effective we might be as adults had we been more imaginatively stimulated to verbalize our world of play when we were children. How often we find we cannot get rid of our frustrations or solve our problems because we cannot lift them to the talking level! We are rigid and tumble our symbols like stiff old men. Students go to the library to look up data on cleft palate speech, for instance. If they find no articles by the title they are stumped. They do not mumble to themselves "cleft palate—speech problem—don't talk well." Thus, they don't think about the implication in the topic of rejection or the self-concept or the body image or feedback or the possibility of talking to strangers like a person with cleft palate in order to learn first hand. All of us, too, seldom see a second way to skin a cat or a problem because we have not verbalized our experiences sufficiently. Thought is not an artesian well; we need to pump thought with speech.

It is in those years between two and seven that we acquire an immense number of words. Everything has a name, and the child drives his elders to distraction for a spell with the incessant question, "What is it?" During this period the child thinks something like the country bumpkin who could not understand how men ever came to know the names of the stars. Who told them? To the child the name becomes an inseparable part of the thing. And by talking with his new words in a variety of combinations he causes them to take on an increasing number of associations. He comes to know what is meant by a sneaky cat, a loud color. If he grows up to be a scientist he will even understand what is meant by "white noise." One small boy said to his grandmother, "I like your voice, Grandma; I wish I could put it around my neck." The preschool child delights in word play, in changing words around, and thus he stirs and patterns his inner processes. Vigotsky reasoned that the gradual silencing of preschool egocentric speech begins the separation of inner and outer speech, and that gradually the child's thought processes lose their resemblance to speech. But we all know, or at least should, that when our thoughts get stuck we need to talk. If you want to solve a problem, talk about it.

Poets babble nonsense in order to regenerate the flow of words once it has been stopped. "Brainstorming," a technique designed to stir up as many solutions to a problem as possible, has become a popular procedure among business executives and even scientists. Students of the brainstorming process state that many of the best solutions come after all the easy answers have been spoken. Problems are problems only because our habitual words are not appropriate. And if we have the fluency to keep churning out other word combinations, after the common ones have been exhausted, we are likely to stumble upon a new view that works. Edison noted in his diary that a light bulb grows dark on the bottom with use, and there he stopped. (He probably should have talked to somebody about it.) In any event, those who noticed the possible relationships involved laid the ground work for the development of the electronic tube, basic in the development of radio and television. Those who imagined and talked about the unseen world of matter as similar to the planets in space developed the atomic theory of protons and electrons. If the microcosm is a macrocosm in miniature, perhaps the dialogue within a man is comparable to the dialogue among men.

This power to make associations, as man does, may be ascribed, at least in part, to the linear nature of language. To speak is to string words like beads; we cannot say two words at a time, or scoop them out, as with a shovel. Words and thoughts must come one at a time, like babies. The perception of the senses, in contrast, is nuclear. We see all the people and furniture in the room at once. We hear the sixty trombones at once, not one after the other. It is the ability to replace and interchange words which form patterned wholes that comprises our supreme analytical power. When we think in words we act very much like a Detroit assembly line, interchanging at will a combination of tops, doors, and other parts, and thus producing sedans, hardtops, coupes, and sports models. Other animals do not have factory production lines, at least in part because they do not have verbal production lines. It is the child's destiny to play with words, shuffling them about, and noting their patterns.

> The top goes on the bottom. The top is the bottom. The bottom is the top. The top does not have a bottom. The bottom-top. Top-bottom. Botop. Topbot. Top top tippity top.

Patterning

We have already spoken of symbolic patterning. Patterning is placing form on the data of thought. Patterning is really the heart of what we call "meaning." When we say, "Oh, I see," what was previously scrambled information now makes sense. Not just a heap of assorted bones, but the "shin bone connects to the knee bone, the knee bone connects to the thigh bone . . ." and then we have a skeleton. Wallas saw this patterning as the third step in the creative act.(16) First, the inclination to explore; second, the associative play or incubation; and third, the sudden structure of the idea. Dewey's "exploration of the possible solutions" and "the selection of the best" recognize this Gestalt step in the thinking process.

Piaget observed that patterning ability developed most notably in the years between seven and puberty.(17) He called it the development of "concrete operational thinking," and the peculiar characteristic he observed at this point in the child's speaking and thinking was his new found capacity to think about objects when the objects were not present to be manipulated. It is one thing to talk about the little toy dog in the store window when the child has his nose pressed against the window, and quite a different thing to talk about the same dog when the child is in bed. Small children are extremely vague in their recollections, and they color their memory efforts with their observations of the moment. The plastic dog in the window may become furry like the bear the child tucks under his arm when he crawls into bed. It is the developing capacity of the seven-year-old *to talk* about the patterned past with increasing accuracy that has freed the human race from the bondage of other animals. To understand how human thought gained its wings is to understand the difference between the verbal language of man and the rudiments of language possessed by the more social nonhuman animals.

The comparison of the symbolic power of man to that of other animals indicates that it is man's peculiar ability to create a vast array of replaceable symbols that lies at the heart of his unique power. Other creatures symbolize action, the predicate part of our sentences, but they have no way of naming things. The dog pokes his nose under the master's arm and lifts it, or runs back and forth between the master and the door, indicating that he wants to get out. The bee dances in one fashion to indicate the nectar is within one hundred yards. If it dances in another style it suggests the approximate number of degrees, from a bearing toward the sun, which the worker bee must fly to come upon the nectar. Many creatures have cries that invite fight or affection or fear or supplication, thus expressing "go away," "come here," "I quake," or "help." In all these illustrations, the infrahuman creature is symbolizing the action expressed in the predicate of a sentence. The dancing bee is acting out nectar hunting, but doing it instinctively, not thoughtfully. The peculiarly limiting feature of animal thought and communication is its lack of facility in representing things. The dog may pick up his plate and bring it to his master or yap in an irritated fashion, but he has no way of specifying "Gravy Train, tonight please." If he does not get what he wants, he does not eat. The master will have to keep trying different foods until the finicky pet eats. The hunting dog will point toward the pheasant. The ape will reach for the banana with the stick. The bee will bring some of the nectar to the hive to indicate what his dancing is about. These are examples of first order nouns. The plate *stands for* food. The pointing *stands for* pheasant, and so forth. But the animal is powerless away from the physical presence of the object he uses for his symbol.(18) Only the very brightest ape finally thinks of the stick in the next room as he alternately slaps the floor in frustation and then stops and drools, all the while looking longingly at the banana high above his head. We may surmise that memory with animals is a function of the immediate environment. As a result, the subhuman animal lives in the present. He is an existentialist philosopher by necessity, not choice. The time scale of yesterday and tomorow—the beginning and eternity—are beyond his reach. Some of our own behavior suggests this pocket of the present within which other animals must live.

> The story is told about a railroad engineer of thirty-five years experience who failed to pass a written test of the rules of the road. His superiors were horrified. Here was a man with the lives of many people in his hands who apparently did not know his job. They called him in and presented him with the facts, to which he answered. "I couldn't make no sense out of that test. Sure I know the rules of the road. How do you suppose I been operating a locomotive? You let me put my hand on the throttle and lean out the cab and I know what to do."

Here is an example illustrating how easy it is to give directions within the range of what can be seen:

> "Can you tell me where Thomson Hall is?"
> "Yes, see the yellow brick over there, next to the corner?"
> "Yes."
> "That's it."

But now let us take an example where a person is trying to give directions to a place at some unseen distance.

> "I am looking for the City Building."
> "It's east of here."
> "You mean I just keep going down this road?"
> "No, this street dead ends. You have to take Darlington south till it runs into Bestow Drive. Then . . ."
> "But where is Darlington?"
> "It's up this way. Look, turn your car around and go the way you came until you come to a stop sign."
> "The first stop sign?"
> "Yes, there is only one."
> "What do you mean, there is only one stop sign?"

> "Just go until you come to a stop sign. Then turn to your left, that's south. Darlington runs. . . ."

So far as we know the poor devil never did find the City Building.

Most of us are unable to follow the instructions for the assemblage of a simple toy, but place the parts in our hands and we can figure out how to put them together—probably because we have not been trained to translate a set of directions. Most of our school testing concerns the retrieval of information that we have read. But it is important to learn how to capture the image of physical things and to be able to talk about them in language that is translatable. We have our speeches of demonstration in many speech classes and they come close to the objective. But we should also give speeches of demonstration *without the visual aids*. It is that capacity to formulate, in speech of precise terms, the laboratory experiment in chemistry you did the day before that trains this unique patterning capacity.

> Vigotsky believed that the telescoping of experience into a noun or two, as in the title of a book, is the essence of the structuring act we are talking about. The connotation of a word, as contrasted to the dictionary meaning, is the packing of that experience into a word. Vigotsky explained that "inner speech" is a telegram, or a kind of poetry, a message meaningful to one person only, the thinker. He believed we experience both "word thought" and "non-word thought." "I wanted to utter a word," he said, "but that word I cannot remember; the bodiless thought will now return to the palace of shadows." Einstein said he did not know in what symbols he did his scientific thinking, that it was only later, when he wanted to talk to another person, that he translated his thought into words. We all know these shifts that begin in bodiless thought, then transform themselves into half-formed phraseology, and finally emerge as meaningful communication. The thinking that erupts finally in structured speech comes out of the telegraphic form of inner speech that is born in mystery.(19)

Man is the one animal that can function quite well in the absence of things. Apparently not fully recognizing the point, Vigotsky takes issue with the biblical statement "In the beginning was the word." In the beginning was the thing, says Vigotsky. We do not agree. At the ape level of existence this may be true, but man is no ape. It is the word that gave man his beginning. Ancient Egypt, Greece, and Rome are gone, but by means of symbols, we are able to hold them (never having experienced them) and to learn from them as from the present. If much of our thinking is sentenceless and often wordless, as indeed it seems to be, it is still by the use of word symbols, rather than of signs standing for things, that we are freed from time and place, to structure and restructure symbols as we jolly well please. This is the foundation of man's power to imagine giants and satyrs and devils, or even our ghostly flight to the moon.

Each man stores his past in verbal patterns, and in verbal patterns he may also contemplate his future. This is of the most profound significance when we contemplate how the child becomes an effective man. A study of the lives of creative people shows that they, by their own accounts, return to the dreams of their childhood, to drink at those springs, when their energy flags and they feel caught in deadening routine. "The thoughts of youth are long, long thoughts," and the grown man must still be able to *verbalize* his early thoughts if he is to continue to grow. Goethe observed that each man in his time, in one fashion or another, works out the dreams of his childhood. Edith Cobb, in her study of great personalities, says that they frequently *tell* of those moments in their childhood, between the ages of seven and thirteen, when they lay in the grass, looked into the heavens and felt the power of comprehending the universe—at once realizing their speck-like proportions.(20) "A considerable speck!" concluded Robert Frost, with Yankee understatement.

We are saying this: That the evidence shows that growth is facilitated by, if not dependent upon, the verbal storing of the pattern of one's experience in words, by the making of commentary on one's experience—as the child does in his play—and by the talking out of the pattern of one's hopes for the future. People who are lost in the sea of life have not talked about their lives. Speech about the self serves as a compass, letting us know from whence we came, our present position, and whither we may tend. The late President Kennedy deeply stirred the nation in no small measure because he had the unique power to verbalize for the nation in electrified tones a cohesive pattern of the past, the present, and the aspired future.

> Our observations of college students is that those who remain immature are those who have not talked to anyone about their lives and possible futures. One Negro boy said he did not know what the word "college" meant until he received several letters in his high school senior year from colleges and universities offering him football scholarships. Even then he was about to throw them

away like soap ads until his father said, "How come? That's money. That's a future." Post high school had meant "a car and better food." "Even after I came, 'college' didn't mean what it does now until I was elected to a student government position. Then I found what *I said* counted. College began to mean a better life for me and my race." An overly protected girl said, "Reality meant where I lived and the people I knew and talked to. Coming to college made Japan and Spain, other places and people, seem real. Everything except my immediate world was abstract. Even violence and corruption were just words we learned, like Asia and South America. And my first reaction to life here at college when it began to seem real was that it was evil, for though now it was real it was different from my little world at home." Both of these students now have promise, most particularly because they can now verbalize their early dream limitations. But the key point to see here is that the great patterns of thought in each life are the designs each person weaves for himself, and this he does because he develops early in life an array of labels that he can manipulate in the absence of the things for which they stand. Surely our education should focus on such things.

"What are patterns for?" asked Amy Lowell. Patterns are designs for things to come, and this is their purpose. Human thought patterns do their essential work when they mold human lives. In this rests the potentialities of the human race. The very core of education is teaching the young to verbalize their experiences and the dreams that emerge, which the listener handles as he would the robes of God.

Reality Testing

When we think, we are propelled by a vague urge to manipulate the symbols aroused, to discover a meaningful pattern among them, and finally to check the pattern to see if it is fact or fancy. Those who think little tend to be comforted by the feeling that they have figured it all out and that they are the realists. They know what's what. "Wot's wot? Ah, it's a wise cove as knows that," growled the pirate in Stevenson's *Treasure Island*. Those who think much suffer the experience of everlastingly discovering the falsity of their evidence and reasoning. But "what would you rather be," asked John Stuart Mill, "a contented pig or a discontented philosopher?" The thinking man discontentedly keeps changing the filters in his mind. Perhaps the hardest lesson to learn, and one a person must learn if he is going to speak with wisdom, is that much of what he knows at any given time may not be true. We speak and work with what we have, and when we must we revise. As learners we accumulate more and more knowledge and skill; as thinkers we change and reshape our knowledge, and this is the thinking skill. As learners we speak as if the truth can be known; as thinkers we speak as if we can never know the ultimate truth. We speak in terms of hypotheses and follow where they lead.

Some philosophers argue that the word "reality" is a symbol for a mental construct, not something out there which we can discover. And maybe it is. But the last step in thinking through something, and the most sophisticated step the child finally attains, is the *testing* of a mental product. "It is this continual reassessment that permits the innovation and novelty of human life,"(21) and therefore it is indispensable to thought.

> From our own experience as both teachers and students of speech we know how easy it is for student speakers to feel their job is done once they have spoken. But if we stop here we learn little. The question-answer period is an excellent way to find out our impact, what we made clear, and where we sank in a swamp. We need to ask our listeners to write out our main purpose, to tell us where we irritated them, to tell us the sentence that struck home, to tell us what we made them think. We need to listen to a recording of our speech, and to *comment* on our experience, how we felt, the surprises we experienced, the nonverbal behavior of the audience, and how well we think we hit the mark. Football teams study films of the last game and scout the future opponent.

Reality testing is extremely painful, however, for it comes at a moment when we are least able to tolerate it. Testing follows that godlike experience of creating life out of dust and detail. If evaluation shows that we have given birth to a low-browed idiot of a brain child, while we, with our defenses down, are still experiencing the exhilaration of our achievement, we stagger as by a blow to the midsection. This is, in part, why criticism following speeches, red marks on papers, and suggestions after any act are extremely hard to take. All action—and particularly speech—when well done, is in large measure unconscious. Self-awareness is submerged when we act. Evaluation brings us back to self-awareness, after unconscious flight, and the shock is great. It is little wonder that only the strongest can afford to think, speak up, and test their thought in the ears of other men.

Summary and Conclusion

We would like to conclude the chapter with some anticipations of the future. Despite the folly of the present human scene, we hold William Faulkner's faith "that man will not merely endure; he will prevail."(22) This hope is our heritage and we must not only pass it on, but seek its fulfillment. We need a vision, however dimly outlined, of those things that in due course must come to pass. Our own private vision is that this society will eventually come to train its young to think more fluently and efficiently and thus to behave in accordance with long term self-interest. Oh, we know how the cynics laugh. "Must we endure one more Utopia?" they ask. But we envisage no perfect society without problems, but rather a world of many men highly similar to our better men of this day and days of the past. The pessimists have brainwashed us into believing that the glands of most men must doom them to evil and self-destruction—that the tail must run the head.

But we still hope, and on the basis of fact as well as inclination. We feel that even now the behavioral sciences are beginning to lay the foundations for a better day. This book was born of our understanding of that research. Many are beginning to see that a new education is on its way, primarily designed to teach our children to be comfortable with their thoughts and feelings and to enjoy thinking instead of anxiously storing a questionable assemblage of information or acquiring a few primitive skills. After all, the course of history is dotted by men who did teach themselves to think and to talk with precision and clarity and beauty.

For us, the most pertinent aspect of the vision is our belief that speech will be the crucial vehicle for this training in thinking. Let us dare to sketch, however vaguely, the manner whereby this may come to be. We believe that the future curriculum will center about speech activities. These will not be the type of speech activities which now dominate our schools. Instead, our children in the home and in the school, will be stimulated in every possible way to pattern experience verbally. Skill in verbal commentary, and prediction as well as recall will receive the rewards. Our children will be trained to be highly fluent in free association, in freewheeling imagining. Their ability to create symbolic patterns of all types will be encouraged daily. They will be taught to evaluate and to revise these patterns and to transform them from one set of symbols into another. For example, children will talk about what they paint and paint what they talk about. Translation and transformation will be stressed.

They will speak many answers to the same question and put them in order of accuracy. Our children of the future will be trained not only to read the thoughts of their authors, but also to paraphrase them simultaneously and, above all else, to attend the thoughts which these generate. They will learn to listen in the same fashion, constantly translating and transforming what they hear into their own private self-talk. They will find that their elders and their teachers will genuinely prize their verbal constructions of new concepts and solutions. Our children will, in short, be rewarded for thinking. Creative speech will get the highest honors.

It may be that we shall never know the intricacies of the relationship between speech and man's crowning powers to comprehend himself and his universe, or even between speech and those skills that will shoot him to the moon. But we do know that in the mystery of human evolvement speech was born, which gives man his uniqueness. In man's beginning was the word. Whatever the source of speech and whatever its relationships to our innermost selves and the universe, it is by speech we have grasped the power to become the human race and to draw the design of the future man to which we may aspire.

7 The Pleasures of Speech

We fear we have been awfully solemn thus far in our discussion of the functions of speech, almost sounding as though speaking had no fun in it. We shall try to make amends in this chapter. For speech has probably as much pleasure in it as any other human function. The baby knows that verbal play is good fun. Watch his babbling and chortling in his crib, making fools of all his elders who answer his sublime nonsense with some of the same. Throughout his life much of his speech will be punctuated with laughter. Animals can't laugh; even the hyena and loon can only cry wildly. A sense of humor is the by-product of speech. Because we can talk, we can laugh.

There is pleasure to be had in all forms of speaking, the formal and the informal alike. Consider how much time we spend just in verbal ping-pong. Much of our conversation is little more than a glorified form of the infant's babbling. We've collected some samples:

> "Whatcha going to do now?"
> "Oh, I dunno. Just take it easy."
> "Take it easy, eh? Won't make any nickels that way."
> "Who wants nickels? I'm a dollar man, myself."
> "Yeah?"
> "Yeah."

Very little comunication in that exchange and not much emotional expression, thought, or social control. Perhaps a bit of egocentric speech, but primarily the speakers are just making verbal faces at each other, making noises. It's fun to make noises, to yak. Some of the pleasure is merely that of togetherness. Man is a herd creature. He does not like to be alone too long. When we talk to each other we know we are not alone. Perhaps we're like whippoorwills. We don't always have to make sense, but we have to answer each other. We need the feeling of joining, of union.

It is fascinating to overhear conversations analytically, especially when they are between strangers. First there are the verbal gestures of recognition; next comes the exploration stage in which each speaker takes turns in revealing himself and probing the other for identity information; then comes the stage of communion, of mutual sharing of familiar experiences; and finally (if the conversation really clicks), the leapfrog stage wherein the two minds now in tune take turns exploring the unfamiliar and the unknown, each stimulating the other.

An example may illuminate. One of the advantages of being a middle-aged professor is the complete invisibility he seems to possess when he invades a student lounge or coffee shop. One quick look, and the students erase him from all consciousness. The other day we heard this conversation in the student union. The two speakers were in their twenties, the girl very attractive and the man very manly. As he drank his coffee, he was drawing some curious pictures in a notebook and the girl was highly aware of his occasional glances in her direction. Finally their eyes met and he grinned:

"Hullo!"

"Hi! Monsieur Picasso, I presume!" She gestured at his drawings.

"No, I run worms. . . ."

"Oh. . . . Who usually wins?" Her eyes twinkled. He grinned.

"I'm a psych major," he explained. "I'm doing a study of how flat worms learn to go through a maze. Guess I'm more lost than they are right now so I guess they've won. . . . What do you do?"

"I tie flies. . . ."

"Oh, come on! Bet they don't like being tied. What knots do you use: bowline or sheepshank?"

"I asked for that," smiled the girl. "I'm really an art major. I guess I said that about tying flies, which really is true and I'm pretty good at it . . . my dad taught me . . . was because the only contact I've ever had with worms is in fishing. I don't like 'em that's why I prefer flyfishing. Why spend your life with worms?"

"I'm not spending my life with worms. I just run them an hour a day as part of my graduate assistantship. I like girls too. Wish I could run them instead. . . ."

"Oh? What sort of a maze would you use for us?"

"One with lots of dead ends." He sensed here that he was stepping into a bog, so he returned to safer ground and continued. "Say, you're an art major. What do you think of my drawing of Jezebel?" he showed her his notebook.

"What's Jezebel?"

"Oh, she's my primadonna worm. She goes only in circles. Really! She just can't run a straight-line maze like all the other flatworms can. Just curls up. But I invented a sort of spiral maze and she. . . ." The girl laughed. "She? Didn't think worms had sex. How do you know if it's a he or she?"

"She's contrary, that's why. . . ."

"You mean she won't do what you want her to. Smart gal, Jezebel. I think I'd like Jezebel. . . ."

"You would? Say, would you like. . . ?

And so it went. Both participants were enjoying themselves hugely, playing with words and ideas, developing a union, stimulating each other. We have known better conversations on both higher and lower levels than that illustrated here, but almost always they seem to follow the same sequence and to have the same dynamics. Good conversation is much more an art than a science, and the attempt to design a conversation upon a formula would doubtless be doomed to failure. Nevertheless, we are certain that conversational ability can be improved in each of us if we try, and that we can have more fun out of it than we realize.

One of the things we must do is to talk more, to different people, about different things, if we wish to attain skill in this poor man's art form. All these parts are important. We have all known the verbal lemon who must be squeezed hard to get even a trickle of conversational juice—often sour stuff at that, or the padlocked person whose combination is known to only a few, or the open-faucet person from whose lips there pours forth a constant stream of the unimportant, the repetitive, and the uninteresting. We need model ourselves after none of these. If we look we can find better models almost anywhere. Or perhaps we need merely to realize the tremendous asset of being an interesting conversationalist, and to develop our own particular variety thereof.

We have said that it is important to talk to different people about different things. One of the best verbal companions we ever knew did not really talk very much himself, but he had an uncanny ability to get others to do so. He was able to strike up a conversation with anyone and to make them talk interestingly. After watching him ply his skills for some time we asked him if he knew how he did it. "Oh, I don't know," he answered.

> I guess I just like people and I know that every single one of them has an interesting anecdote if I can only wheedle it out of him. And often, once that one comes out, it's only the first, like beads on a string. No one can live in this world for very long without having some interesting things happen to him, or without making some observations that I can enjoy. I've learned more from people than I ever did from you professors or your books, and I've had a ball doing it. How do I do it? I guess I'm interested in whatever they tell me.

But he had more than mere interest. First of all, he was a free, outgoing person, free enough to run the small risk of being rejected if he opened up the conversation. Then he always revealed himself by some casually humorous remark or anecdote. From that point onward, he merely reflected in his own words, but with obvious appreciation, whatever his victims told him. He would have made a tremendously successful counseling psychologist or psychiatrist. We know because every time he talked to us he milked us of personal information we had not remembered or shared with another person for years. Only afterward were we able to realize that we had done almost all the talking. Yet the impression remains: he was one of the best conversationalists we have ever met.

Perhaps we always like conversational partners who get us to use the monologue. Certainly we do not gain much pleasure in conversation with the verbal vultures who hover over anything we are saying, waiting impatiently for any opportunity to swoop down and grab the topic away from us, often not waiting at all but interrupting or demonstrating their complete disinterest in the fascinating things we are expounding. This is not to say that good conversation is merely a seesaw of monologues. The candy of speech is not evenly divided. Indeed, conversation is always uneven, never truly balanced. But any true sharing, which is always what good conversation entails, requires some consideration for the partner. There are times when one person should do most of the talking while the other's role should be confined to appreciation and reinforcement through the little questions or echoes of encouragement, playing Boswell to Samuel Johnson. After all, this is how most women capture their men for life. They get them to talking about themselves at length, at much length, and before the poor male knows what has happened, he has told her so much he has to marry her to protect himself. "Aw," he says. "At last I've found someone who understands and appreciates me." Yes, indeed, and for the preservation of the species it is probably well that he does not know that she shall have her turn at the conversation, yea, all the remaining years of their life, until death do them part.

If you want your share of the conversation, learn to tell an anecdote well. People always listen to them. The story teller has always been favored not only in our own infancy when we sat on our mother's knee, or in the infancy of the race, but always. A good raconteur can grace any gathering, can give a dead party life. The ability to tell a tale well often appears to be a gift from the genes or genii, but it's more a learned discipline than a gift. Every word must be programmed with care to develop the pattern so that it will be most effective. A good story is almost a sonnet. The first few times you tell it, unless you have stolen it from another skilled story teller and have total recall, the production will have many flaws. There will be too many words in the wrong places and inappropriate ones in the right places. It's so easy to spoil the effect by a few extra sentences. The skill is not easily achieved, but most of us can manage it if only we can find enough ears to belabor with our practicing.

Your authors, in their consultation for this book, have examined their personal repertoire of anecdotes and stories for possible illustrative inclusion here. Both of us are experienced public speakers and we have told many a tale in the course of our professional lives, some of them true, some of them embellished with what Gilbert and Sullivan called "corroborative detail intended to give artistic verisimilitude to a bald and unconvincing narrative."

One of us wanted to put in the story of Mary, the untactful little girl who always said the wrong thing, constantly embarrassing her parents. It seems that the preacher was coming to call one afternoon and that he had a big nose, a huge beak of a nose. And the mother was deathly afraid that Mary would say something about it. So she told the girl, "Now, Mary, when the preacher comes, all you say, and I mean all, is 'How do you do, Reverend Jones. I have to go to bed now,' and then you do it. He has a big nose, but don't you dare say anything about it. He can't help it. Now remember, don't say anything else." Well, Mary promised and the preacher came and as the mother was pouring the preacher's tea, Mary stuck her head in the door and focused her eyes on the minister's nose. "How . . . how . . . how do you do, Reverend Jones?" she greeted him. "I have to . . . hey, Mummy, do I have to?" "Yes Mary, go to bed. Upstairs, right now." Mary withdrew, still with her eyes on the preacher's nose. From the landing, she called, "Mummy . . . I . . . I. . . ." "Get upstairs, this minute, Mary. And Reverend Jones, how many lumps of sugar would you like in your nose?"

Your authors decided to skip such horrible examples. "There are only seven good stories in the world," said Mark Twain, "And six of them you dare not tell the ladies." We've been hunting for that seventh one. If you find it, let us know.

The personal anecdote is safer and does not need to be quite so well polished since your listener is as much interested in what it says about you as he is in the occurrence itself. The only danger in telling of a personal experience is that it may have merely personal meaning, and the listener will be unable to identify enough to share it with you. If you are empathizing with your listener as you should, you will know when you are inviting boredom. But we must not forget that these anecdotes are usually of great listener interest, and that each of us has them to offer. "Got a million of 'em," said Jimmy Durante. Most of us have enough for almost any conversation if only we take the trouble to remember those which have interested others in the past.

Let us tell you an experience of one of the authors. You probably will not believe it, but it's true. It happened many years ago when he was a graduate assistant.

I was helping a Hindu wise man get a picture of the soul. Dr. T., the director of the department of psychopathology where I was employed, walked up to me one day and without any preliminaries said, "As of this instant, I'm relieving you of all your duties. Shackson will take care of your left-handed rats, Charles Hazzard will finish building that amplifier, and Hilden can measure the rest of those Achilles' tendon reaction times." My face fell. It was the post-Depression year, 1932, and my fifty dollars a month research assistantship was all I had to live on while I struggled to complete my doctorate in psychology: fifty dollars and the carrots, lettuce, and the occasional steak I smuggled from the hospital icebox where I procured the milk for my experimental animals. I was wondering which cook had betrayed me when the director smiled. "No, you're not being fired. I just have another assignment for you—an important one. I want you to photograph the soul." He grinned evilly.

As we walked back to his laboratory in the university psychopathic hospital, he explained. A famous Hindu savant named Kima had heard of our pioneering researches with brain waves and action currents. He had come to our university, all the way from India, because he was convinced that these electrical currents might reveal the soul in action. "I tried to tell him that these waves of electrical potential that sweep across the cortex of the brain or accompany muscular effort are physiological, not spiritual, processes," said the director, "but he won't listen. When I showed him some of our photographs of action currents he started talking nonsense about soul pictures, or something. I've been instructed by the President of the University to show this man every courtesy, so he's all yours, son. You'll find him in the next office. Photograph his bloody soul but keep him out of my hair."

I spent most of my waking hours for three months with Kima. They were good months, for Kima was both interesting and intelligent. He mastered every shred of information about these brain waves and action currents, and insisted that I do likewise so that he could discuss them with me. And then, when he found I could not understand his all-consuming hunger to find the spirit or soul, he began to teach me a bit of the strange wisdom of the East. Then he insisted that I learn seven postures. My knees creaked and my legs went to sleep and my thoughts kept shifting from Karma to a girl called Katie. I sure was relieved when Kima finally evolved an experimental design.

According to Kima, the soul is active when a person is inactive but alert and attentive or imagining. So to get at its essence, all muscular activity has to cease, because that masks the soul's action. When I protested that, if this were so, the only way we could get a picture of the pure soul was to kill the subject, Kima agreed. I then suggested that he ask the director to be our first experimental animal. As always, Kima made me ashamed of my irreverent levity. He patiently explained that, of course, we could not kill our experimental subjects, as logical as such a procedure would seem, but that perhaps by reducing the amount of muscular activity we might be able to recognize dimly the soul's essential features. It would only be necessary to have our subjects thoroughly quiet.

So I built my apparatus. It consisted of a padded chair with arms. On one arm there was a narrow carriage built of wood. The subject's arm was to be placed on this. This was attached near the back of the chair so that it could be swung up and down, bending the subject's arm at the elbow. You see, by means of a motor and a rope working over some pulleys, the arm carriage could be lifted without the subject's effort. Electrodes were to be placed over the critical spots on the subject's lifting muscles so that any tiny action currents in those muscles could be detected and photographed on our oscilloscope. The night before we began the experiment, I went over to the lab and painted the whole thing with pure white enamel. Somehow the bare wood and screws didn't quite seem appropriate for catching the human soul. I also attached a small temple gong, which Kima had given me, to the top of the contraption so that when the arm carriage pointed straight up, the gong would clang. Kima smiled when he saw it. He said that it was my essential reverence, not my irreverence, which had compelled me to make these changes.

Our laboratory was in the basement of the psychopathic hospital, right under the ward where they kept the female patients who were highly disturbed. It was not a very quiet place except at meal time, so we chose noon to give the experiment its first dry run. The procedure was as follows. After the subject was placed in the padded chair with his right arm in the carriage and the wires attached to the muscles, the subject was to lift the arm in the carriage slowly to the vertical or gong position. Then drop it. Next he was to let the arm remain passive as the motor lifted the arm till the gong sounded. Then, he was merely to imagine that the arm was being lifted; and finally, he was to imagine that he was lifting the arm. Then we would repeat the four steps in the reverse order. It was Kima's hope that the third and fourth steps or conditions would be the ones which would reveal the essential features of the soul in action, for these were the ones where attentive imagination alone would be present.

I had expected that Kima would desire to be the subject, but he was very firm in his refusal. "I have searched for this for forty years," he said. "I am close to my dream but it is not for me to see my own soul." So saying, he went into one of his trance-like states of meditation and I went out for a hamburger. When I returned, he hooked me up in the chair and started the cameras whirring. I raised my arm; I had my arm raised; I imagined both. I did them again in reverse order. Then Kima disengaged the camera and although I was skeptical, I felt a curious flare of excitement as we went into the darkroom to develop the films.

All eight shots looked alike! Those taken when I was imagining showed action currents not as large in amplitude, but that was the only difference. There was no profile of a soul. I made some sad joke about having lost my soul to Satan last Homecoming night, and suggested that we try it on the director's secretary who I was sure had as beautiful a soul as she had legs. I also proposed that we put her leg in the carriage instead of her arm, but that was vetoed by both Kima and the young lady. So we used her arm. Again the films showed a result similar to my own. I regarded the secretary with renewed interest: perhaps she didn't have a soul either. Kima was neither amused nor discouraged. "We should not expect to see the soul so easily," he said. "I must mediate upon this thing."

The next day, his face was all bright. "I now know why we failed," he said. "It is because you Americans are never still; you are never quiet. What we have found on these films is your constant tension. It has masked the features of the soul. I must teach you to be quiet so that your souls can be seen. When you have learned how to be at peace within your skin, we shall make a new recording."

So with five others, including the secretary who was getting more beautiful all along, I was chosen to learn Kima's method of relaxation. He said it was a variant of Yoga. He said he practiced it every day of his life and that that was why his face had no wrinkles in it—which was true. He told me he was fifty-four years old, but he had the face of a ten-year-old. There in the dusty basement laboratory, Kima trained us in Yoga relaxation. First, he sat the six of us in chairs with our right arms resting on the table. Then he told us to roll our eyeballs upward and backward—"the position of death and peace." Then, while maintaining this, we had to close our eyelids over the eyeballs and to exhale just a bit further than usual, then end the exhalation with a tiny silent sigh. Over and over again he trained us until we could follow the sequence at will. Finally he was satisfied with our performance.

"Now," said Kima, "I must tell you the last step, the heart-secret of relaxation. The eyeballs backward, the long breathe out, these are essential, but there is this also: you must come to see life as a whole. In my Yoga, the whole is the circle. In my body the circle is my navel. You must then also see life as a whole. Meditate upon your navel."

Not a one of us ever learned to relax the Yoga way. Everytime we thought of our navels our eyeballs went down. Kima gave up and went back to India. Sometimes, remembering my lost youth, I ring the gong for him.

All right. You've had your illustration of how to tell a personal story and we have had our vulgar indulgence. We do not know how much you have enjoyed it as a piece of reading, but there have been times when we were able to tell it well to a group about a fireside. Some students will say, "But things like that have never happened to me. I have nothing to tell." We doubt you. We are certain that already you have had experiences that would fascinate us, and moreover that you will have many more. But you must recognize them, store them for future use, and bring them out when the situation is appropriate and tell them well. Must you save your anecdotes for your dotage? We would bet that if we had the chance, and the appropriate situation to disarm you, that we could evoke from you experiences that would be just as interesting, if not as strange. Every life has its stories. The thing is to recognize them and to share them and to develop their telling with skill. It's fun to have good conversation and it's fun to tell stories, and good for the human soul, even though, as you have learned, it is difficult to photograph.

But the pleasures of speech do not belong only to the fireside, student center, or social event. Pleasure in speech can and should be a part of everyday experience, and certainly it should be a part of the speech course itself. It is really too bad that so many students enroll in a speech course because they know they have to or because they think they ought to. Few of them ever take it for sheer pleasure, and we admit that few of them undergo the experience and remember it as 100 per cent fun. Piano playing isn't all fun either. Nevertheless, most students who manage, even in the first course, to get enough bits of reward to enable them to know ease and security within the speaking situation, should be tempted to take another course or two in the field. We always hope they will, because we know what they do not—that advanced speech courses can be pleasurable indeed.

Let us sketch briefly the pleasures that await you. For example, in the class dealing with group discussion, you will find, we hope, the real pleasure that comes from acting as a catalyst. A group of brains are always better than one brain, if only they can be made to mesh, and anyone who has the ability to take a collection of individual personalities and to weld them into a smoothly functioning group will enjoy a sense of both skill and power that few men know. Group discussion is in essence formalized conversation, and you already like to converse. Discussion is purposeful, however, not directionless. The group is focused about a single topic or problem. The trick is to keep them so focused. A good group leader or even a participant often plays a shepherd's role. Indeed, it is everybody's task (often unassumed) to keep the flock moving in the desired direction; there are always laggards to prod; there are always a few strays that obstinately want to take off into the hills; often the rest mill around and bump heads. To help such a motley assemblage and to keep them moving to where they've got to go is a skill of high order, a skill and a craft, almost an art.

The analogy, of course, is imperfect because they are not sheep but human beings, but this makes the achievement all the greater. It's thrilling to belong to such a group as well as to mold it. One feels more than oneself. As a member of a team, we find our individual powers magnified. We get that sense of union in a common task—*e pluribus unum.*

Or you might be interested in exploring the pleasures of a course in public speaking. Throughout the history of our civilization men have sought this training. It was a major part of the education of the ancient Greeks, and is equally satisfying now. What are the pleasures of speaking to an audience? There are many. First, and we admit it with some diffidence, is the ego enhancement. To capture an audience, to bend them to your will, to influence them is the pleasure of power. It is the pleasure of the conductor of a symphony orchestra. The snake charmer in you plays his flute and the audience sways to his bidding. We are not very comfortable in mentioning this, but we have sensed this pleasure deep in our own bones and we have found it good even though we do not admire it. There is a little of the Pied Piper in each of us.

But there are other pleasures too in addressing an audience. There is the joy of artistic creation. You will have prepared for your speeches, gathered your data, shaped and assembled it with care, hunted for just the right words and phrases and ideas that might ring gongs in your audience, ached and suffered a bit in anticipation. And then comes the moment, up there on the platform, where you are on your own, alone. And from your lips there comes an amazing succession of fluent ideas carrying your message to those below. You grab the audience; you make them listen. You move them. You are an artist creating an intricate pattern of the most subtle stuff on earth, a pattern of spoken words. To see your preparation find fulfillment, to sense the electrical excitement, to hear the chuckles, the hum, the little signals of approval, to find that what you have created is applauded, ah, this is good. There are better pleasures than those of the flesh.

Most of us like to argue—and we do a lot of it. It's good fun to wrestle with an opponent, especially when you can win occasionally. Most of you probably have found it difficult to understand why some of your fellow students go out for debate. You see them in the library beating their brains, you hear them rehearsing, you see them exhausted, and you wonder why they do it. Well, there are real pleasures to be found in this activity too, pleasures which are probably augmented by the arduous work which it entails. This is what one student debater told us when we asked him what he got out of it:

> It's hard to say. There's the joy of competition of course. Perhaps that comes first. And the killer instinct! To beat the other guy's arguments down, to show that what he says makes no sense, to get him in a corner and destroy his argument, I like that. Doesn't sound very nice, does it, but I sure get a charge out of hanging them on the horns of a dilemma. Of course, I also get it too sometimes. You don't always win. But it's the fun of combat, knowing you've got good weapons, that there's someone out to get you and you'd better get him first. Man against man. It's like prize fighting.

Not all debaters would put this pleasure first. For some, there is the pleasure of disciplining one's thought, the marshaling of arguments, the fitting of them into a logical pattern so they build up to a crescendo of impact. For them, much of the pleasure lies in the strategy, in the countermoves, in the overall design of the presentation. But for all, there is the feeling of companionship that comes from working intimately together in a small group with a close relationship to the coach, the feeling of belonging to a team, the shared experiences of long trips. Debating must be fun or there wouldn't be any.

All of us, at the appropriate times, get pleasure from reciting something we have memorized. It may be a quotation that has some special appeal and pertinence to the moment or a snatch of poetry or some lilting limerick, but there's a pleasure to be found in recitation. Most of us do not do it very well, some unfortunately relying on the cup that cheers to dull our senses enough to be able either to do it or to stand it. We rarely find a bull-chested football player in our oral interpretation classes though you may hear him roaring a bit of "Casey at the Bat" on the bus back to the college after the game. It's too bad. There are real pleasures to be found in reading aloud, and reciting aloud, and the better you can do them the more pleasure you will have.

It takes an experience such as listening to the Lunts or the Laughtons or some other artist of the vocal instrument for us to realize the artistry of human speech. To encase the crucial essence of life in an envelope of words and intonations is no small feat. And the words need not be ours. Others may have expressed the feelings in words better than we ever could, but by saying those words again to another person or an audience, we can make them live and make them our own. For oral interpretation is more than mouthing someone else's utterances. It is a creative act much like that of the violin virtuoso. He plays the notes written on the musical score but he plays them with a difference, his own difference. He takes the production of the composer and makes it his own. To use the voice as an instrument, to stress by intonation and pause the subtle meanings that perhaps even the author never knew, has in it all the deep pleasure of creation. And there is also the applause—no small reward.

You may agree to all this and yet object. You may say, "But I shall never be a virtuoso." This may be true, in part, but you will have moments, those wonderful moments when you have read or recited something well. And, at least, by immersing yourself as you must in a passage, you will make it your own. The rhythm of the thing, like magic, will help you say your own best thoughts more effectively on another day. Few possessions will endure so long.

Again, as in public address, so in oral interpretations, we find the pleasure of power. Using the words of others, it is possible to enthrall, to mesmerize your listeners. You can almost see it happen before your eyes. They lose themselves. For a moment they escape into the world of fantasy that you create. They are yours. But there is also the better joy of sharing. It is not enough to read something that excites or inspires you. Your pleasure is quadrupled when you can share it with others and find that they feel the same impact. Again, you are not alone. You have companions who think and feel as you do. You feel the communion of mankind. You are not alone.

Then there's that strangest of all speech pleasures—talking to an audience that isn't there—the pleasures of radio and television. You screw up your face and smile at the microphone and talk to the vast unknown. It is pleasure indeed to have your voice capture the magical skill that makes it sound to many as if it were meant for each alone. There's soul-catching for you! Again, here we have the pleasure of power. To broadcast is to feel the power of the author, to cast yourself upon the waters, to reach out to people you shall never see, to know you have become entangled in hundreds of lives. It is not all power, either—it's sharing yourself, it's sending your voice afar. Most of us enjoy carving our initials on a tree at some far off point we visited. We carve with our voices too.

Here we find a demand for great art and imagination. Those who work interminable hours in a gadget-filled studio must conjure audiences and imagine their responses. They often wear headphones to help them be the listener, and thus the better speaker. Hidden in the experience is the excitment of turning into art what all men enjoy, the pleasure of being one's most enchanted listener. A tough racket, a ratrace against time, a deadline every minute. It's easy to become addicted.

We also invite you to the pleasures of the theater. No man is complete who has not savored them. When you were a child you tasted them often and found them good, and it seems tragic that as adults so many of us lose ourselves in the day's labor and forget the play. There must be deep pleasure in the drama, for men have participated in it ever since the dawn of history.

What we offer here is not only the vicarious satisfactions of the person in the audience, but also the real fun of taking part in the drama itself. We find it hard to describe, for it is truly a unique experience to be in a play. Often, as we look back on all the agony and effort, we can hardly believe it was worthwhile. Yet we know it was; we know it deep down, and we know that if we have the chance, we may do it again. It's hard to keep away from it once you've known the experience.

But what are the pleasures? First, and probably foremost to the student, is the deep sense of companionship and fraternity that comes from working on the production of a play. There are the late hours, the exhaustion, the hundred crises that must be met, the problems that must be solved jointly, for you are a member of a crew. Formerly lost in the vast anonymity of college, you find an immensely satisfying membership in a closely knit group. Close friendships are forged in the stress and excitement of working together, in mutual creation. Emotions are laid bare but they are shared. Weaknesses are revealed, but all the others involved show their support. You lose yourself in the group, in the play. The play's the thing! You get to know each other intimately. You get to know your instructor, the director. You see him with a hammer banging at a set. You see him undressed of his academic garments, acting out the various parts as he suggests another way to do it. You sense his intense drive and you find yourself responding. You are a member; you are not alone.

There is also the pleasure in the craft itself. After the long rehearsing, both alone and with the others, for once you are really fluent; for once you say the right words with the right voice and the right postures at the right time. It's hard to do, but for once in your life you have done it. To manage this, there must be the intense scrutiny of the language itself, the meanings of the intonations and pauses, the pacing and the emphasis. There is the pleasure of precise timing, of picking up the cue at exactly the right moment, of responding perfectly. It is good to feel yourself the master of your instrument.

But there is also the thrill of seeking excellence. Over and over again you and your fellows play a scene. You know the ache of the last-second flaw that spoils the perfection, but you try again. And then there comes the feeling that all of you are clicking, the exhilaration of making words come alive; the interchanges sparkle, and suddenly everything is just as if you were brilliantly conversing. And then everything is wrong and you start over again, trying, trying always to capture the will-o'-the-wisp of excellence.

The pitch and tempo of the preparation increase as the day approaches. Finally, the audience is out there beyond the curtain.

You won't show it perhaps, but the excitement is almost unbearable. What kind of an audience? Will they like what you, all of you, have forged in such heat and with such labor? Will they? Then up goes the curtain and the play unfolds. Out of the darkness that holds the audience you hear the chuckles, you stop for their guffaws; at just the right moment you freeze in a posture and hold them transfixed in deadly silence. And then suddenly it is over. Applause! Excited talk and shaking hands. "You were great. We did it. Damned if we didn't do it after all!" Then the letdown and the miserable thought, "Can we do it again tomorrow night?" Most of the higher pleasures are outlined in sweet agony; that of the theater is no exception.

We have spoken elsewhere about the need for exploration of new roles in the search for identity. Here let us speak of the pleasures. When you play a part in a play, or speak on the platform, you assume a new identity, you take on a new character. The pleasure lies not in the mere escape from the humdrum self with all its limitations that you know so well. You will feel some of this freedom and it is good, but much better is the gradual realization that taking on a new role enriches you. You grow. No one has ever really played a new role well without finding that somehow he has changed. Here is what on girl said:

> I didn't want to play the part of that evil old woman. I didn't want to become her, not even for the play. I resisted, as you know. But, as I learned to play it, to feel and say the ugly things I had to say, I found a curious experience of growing . . . and, strangely, of being more secure. I've always been afraid of the evil in me, perhaps, but I've hidden it, denied it. And here I was displaying it for all to see . . . at the end almost enjoying it. But I don't think it will make me evil. It's just that I know life will change me and I've been afraid that maybe the ugly side of me may dominate. But here I've found that I can change and yet remain the same, that I can show my ugliness for a moment and yet not remain ugly forever. I'm not afraid of that evil old woman in me anymore.

Probably no one has ever played a part in a theatrical production without some such benefit. We continue to play that part of the part that fits our changing self. Some residue always remains when the final curtain has descended—or as we walk off the platform, having given a speech.

As we bring these descriptions and this book to a close, we do not wish to leave you with the impression that we think that the pleasures of speech are to be found only in speech courses and related activities. It's fun to argue over the coffee table, to talk to any group, to tell a story or an anecdote well, to read aloud to a companion beside the fire, and to "ham it up" a little anywhere. And surely the best of all pleasures is in discovering ever new horizons on the journey of life, a pleasure we owe to the light of speech. What we hope we have done is to help you understand a bit better that the speech we accept so casually is a powerful tool and a priceless possession. This is the stuff that holds you together and holds the world intact.

References

Chapter 1

(1) Wilder Penfield and Lamar Roberts, *Speech and Brain Mechanisms* (Princeton: Princeton University Press, 1959).
(2) R. Ringel, "Some Effects of Tactile and Auditory Alterations on Speech Output" (Ph.D. thesis, Purdue University, 1962).
(3) Elbert R. Moses, "Palatography and Speech Improvement," *Journal of Speech Disorders*, IV (1939), 121–23.

Chapter 2

(1) Daisetz Teitaro Susuki, *Introduction to Zen Buddhism* (New York: The Macmillan Company, 1948), p. 18.

Chapter 3

(1) M. Henle and M. B. Hubbel, "Egocentricity in Adult Conversation," *Journal of Social Psychology*, IX (1938), 222–34.

Chapter 4

(1) *The Writings of Oliver Wendell Holmes* (Boston: Houghton Mifflin Company, 1892), VIII, 293.
(2) Alex Bavelas, "Communication Patterns in Task-Oriented Groups," *Journal of the Acoustical Society of America*, XXII (1950), 725–30; George A. Heise and George A. Miller, "Problem Solving in Small Groups Using Various Communication Nets," *Journal of Abnormal and Social Psychology*, XLVI (1951), 327–35; Harold J. Leavitt, *Managerial Psychology* (Chicago: University of Chicago Press, 1958).
(3) Robert Katz calls this "understanding empathy," Martin Buber calls it "inclusion," Kenneth Burke calls it "identification," Theodor Reik calls it "reverberation."

(4) Cf. Helen V. McKenna, Peter R. Hofstaetter, and James P. O'Connor, "The Concepts of the Ideal Self and of the Friend," *Journal of Personality*, XXIV (1956), 262–71; Josephine Klein, *The Study of Groups* (London: Routledge & Kegan Paul, Ltd., 1956), p. 106; Marvin Sussman, *Sourcebook in Marriage and the Family* (Boston: Houghton Mifflin Company, 1963).
(5) Robert Katz, *Empathy* (New York: The Free Press of Glencoe, Inc., 1963), Chapter II.
(6) James G. Miller, "Some Implications of Communication Theory for Higher Education," *Current Issues in Higher Education*, Association of Higher Education, ed. G. Kerry Smith (Washington, D.C.: Association for Higher Education, 1963), pp. 237–40.
(7) Charles Percy Snow, *The Two Cultures: and a Second Look* (Cambridge, England: Cambridge University Press, 1964).
(8) Harry Stack Sullivan, *The Psychiatric Interview*, eds. Helen Swick Perry and Mary Ladd Gawel (New York: W. W. Norton & Company, Inc., 1954), Chapter V.
(9) G. L. Mangan, D. Quartermain, and G. M. Vaughan, "Taylor MAS and Group Conformity Pressure," *Journal of Abnormal and Social Psychology*, LXI (1960), 146–47.
(10) Rensis Likert, *New Patterns of Management* (New York: McGraw-Hill Book Company, 1961).
(11) C. E. Wells and H. G. Wolfe, "Electrographic Evidence of Impaired Function of Chronically Anxious Patients," *Science*, XXXI (1960), 1671–72.
(12) Leon Festinger, Stanley Schachter, and Kurt Back, *Social Pressures in Informal Groups* (New York: Harper and Row, Publishers, 1950), pp. 413–44.
(13) Harold D. Lasswell and Abraham Kaplan, *Power and Society: A Framework for Political Inquiry* (New Haven: Yale University Press, 1950), Chapters III and X.
(14) Robert F. Bales, A. Paul Hare, and Edgar F. Borgatta, "Structure and Dynamics of Small Groups: A Review of Four Variables," in Joseph B. Gittler, ed., *Review of Sociology: Analysis of a Decade* (New York: John Wiley & Sons, Inc., 1957), pp. 391–422.
(15) Theodore M. Mills, "Power Relations in Three-Person Groups," *American Sociological Review*, XVIII (1953), 351–57.
(16) Robert F. Bales and Edgar F. Borgatta, "Size of Group as a Factor in the Interaction Profile," in A. Paul Hare, *et al.* eds., *Small Groups: Studies in Social Interaction* (New York: Alfred A. Knopf, Inc., 1955), pp. 396–413.

Chapter 5

(1) Joseph Church, *Language and the Discovery of Reality* (New York: Random House, Inc., 1961), p. 62.
(2) Arnold S. Gebel, "Self-perception and Leaderless Group Discussion Status," *Journal of Social Psychology*, XL (1954), 309–18; Paul H. Mussen and Lyman W. Porter, "Personal Motivations and Self-Conceptions Associated with Effectiveness and Ineffectiveness in Emergent Groups," *Journal of Abnormal and Social Psychology*, LIX (1959), 23–27.
(3) Fillmore Sanford, "Research on Military Leadership," in John C. Flanagan, *et al.*, *Psychology in the World Emergency* (Pittsburgh: University of Pittsburgh Press, 1952), pp. 17–74.

(4) Franklyn S. Haiman, "Concepts of Leadership," *Quarterly Journal of Speech,* XXXIX (1953), 317–22; Terence K. Hopkins, "The Exercise of Influence in Small Groups," (Doctoral Dissertation, Columbia University, 1959).

(5) John Dewey has classified work under the following heads: (1) locating the problem, (2) defining the problem, (3) considering the possible solutions, (4) selecting one, (5) testing it by "overt or imaginative action." These are discussed in *How We Think* (Boston: D. C. Heath & Company, 1933), p. 107.

(6) Bernard Berelson and Gary A. Steiner, *Human Behavior: An Inventory of Scientific Findings* (New York: Harcourt, Brace & World, Inc., 1964), p. 666.

(7) Cecil Gibb, "Leadership," in Gardner Lindzey, ed., *Handbook of Social Psychology* (Cambridge, Mass: Addison-Wesley Publishing Company, 1954), pp. 877–920.

(8) Franklyn S. Haiman, "An Experimental Study of the Effects of Ethos in Public Speaking," *Speech Monographs,* XVI (1949), 190–202; Stanley Paulson, "The Effects of the Prestige of the Speaker and Acknowledgement of Opposing Arguments on Audience Retention and Shift of Opinion," *Speech Monographs,* XXI (1954), 267–271; Carl I. Hovland, Irving L. Janis, and Harold H. Kelley, *Communication and Persuasion: Psychological Studies of Opinion Change:* (New Haven: Yale University Press, 1953), pp. 297–299; Paul F. Lazarsfeld, Bernard Berelson, and Hazel Gaudet, *The People's Choice* (New York: Duel, Sloan and Pearce, Inc., 1944), p. 158.

(9) Bernard Berelson and Gary A. Steiner, *Human Behavior: An Inventory of Scientific Findings,* Chapter 17.

(10) Franklin H. Knower, "Experimental Studies of Changes in Attitudes—I, A Study of the Effect of Oral Argument on Changes of Attitudes," *The Journal of Social Psychology,* VI (1935), 315–47.

(11) I & E Division, U.S. War Department, "The Effects of Presenting One Side Versus Both Sides in Changing Opinions on a Controversial Subject," in Newcomb, Hartley, *et al., Readings in Social Psychology* (New York: Holt, Rinehart & Winston, Inc.), pp. 566–77.

(12) Arthur A. Lumsdaine and Irving L. Janis, "Resistance to 'Counterpropaganda' Produced by a One-Sided Versus a Two-Sided 'Propaganda' Presentation," in Carl I. Hovland, Irving L. Janis, and Harold H. Kelley, *Communication and Persuasion* (New Haven: Yale University Press, 1953), pp. 108–11.

(13) Hermann Rauschning, *The Revolution of Nihilism* (Chicago: Alliance Book Corp., 1939), p. 48.

(14) William W. Sargant, *Battle for the Mind* (New York: Doubleday & Company, Inc., 1957).

(15) Richard S. Crutchfield, "Conformity and Character," *American Psychologist,* X (1955), 191–98.

(16) William S. Verplanck, "The Control of the Content of Conversation: Reinforcement of Statements of Opinion, "*Journal of Abnormal and Social Psychology,* LI (1955), 668–76.

(17) Robert R. Blake and Jan S. Mouton, "The Experimental Investigation of Interpersonal Influence," in Albert D. Biderman and Hubert Zimmer, eds., *The Manipulation of Human Behavior* (New York: John Wiley & Sons, Inc., 1961), p. 231.

(18) From a letter in *Life* (Dec. 23, 1946), written by R. S. Aldrich.

(19) Colin W. Turnbull, *The Lonely African* (New York: Doubleday & Company, Inc., 1963).

Chapter 6

(1) Brewster Ghiselin, ed., *The Creative Process* (New York: The New American Library of World Literature, Inc., 1955), p. 233.
(2) Edward Sapir, *Culture, Language and Personality* (Berkeley: University of California Press, 1958); Benjamin L. Whorf, *Language, Thought and Reality*, edited by John B. Carroll (New York: John Wiley & Sons, Inc., 1956).
(3) Joshua Whatmough, *Language, A Modern Synthesis* (New York: The New American Library of World Literature, Inc., 1956).
(4) Jon Eisenson, J. Jeffrey Auer, and John V. Irwin, *The Psychology of Communication*, Chapter 8.
(5) Helen Keller, *The Story of My Life* (New York: Doubleday & Company, Inc., 1954), p. 257.
(6) *Ibid.*, p. 36.
(7) Joseph Church, *Language and the Discovery of Reality*, p. 5.
(8) Frederick C. Bartlett, *Remembering* (New York: The Macmillan Company, 1932).
(9) Recent studies of the first experiences of nonhuman animals indicate that much which we have ascribed to instinct results from previously unobserved earliest happenings. The duckling, for instance, will follow the first moving object that captures its attention. Most ducklings follow their mothers because their mothers are the most likely first moving objects in their lives.
(10) John Bowlby, *Maternal Care and Mental Health* (Geneva, Switzerland: World Health Organization, 1952), Chapter 4.
(11) Kurt Goldstein, *Human Nature in the Light of Psychopathology* (Cambridge, Mass.: Harvard University Press, 1947), p. 41.
(12) Harry F. Harlow, Margaret K. Harlow, and Donald R. Meyer, "Learning Motivated by a Manipulation Drive," *Journal of Experimental Psychology*, XL (1950), 228–34.
(13) C. J. Warden, *Animal Motivation Studies: The Albino Rat* (New York: Columbia University Press, 1931).
(14) Dr. William Dement of Stanford University and Dr. Edward Walpest of Chicago's Medical Rees Hospital and others have found comparable results.
(15) Erich Fromm, *The Forgotten Language* (New York: Holt, Rinehart & Winston, Inc., 1951).
(16) Graham Wallas, *The Art of Thought* (New York: Harcourt, Brace & World, Inc., 1926).
(17) Jean Piaget, *The Construction of Reality in the Child*, trans. Margaret Cook (New York: Basic Books, Inc., Publishers, 1954). Psychologists generally accept Piaget's observations about the steps in child thought development. Recent educational experimentation shows, however, that many children develop the stages more rapidly than Piaget suggests.
(18) Recent anthropological study of animals in their natural environments suggests we may eventually need to modify this generalization.
(19) Lev S. Vigotsky, "Thought and Speech," *Psychiatry*, II (1939), 29–52.
(20) Edith Cobb, "The Ecology of Imagination in Childhood," *Daedalus*, LXXXVIII (1959), 537–48.
(21) Anselm L. Straus, *Mirrors and Masks* (New York: Free Press of Glencoe, Inc., 1959), p. 26.
(22) William Faulkner, from his Nobel speech in 1949.

Index

Index